Arm in Arm

Poems

Catharine Savage Brosman, one of the greatest poets of our age, has recovered for contemporary poetry a concern for the essentially human and universal within a romantic poetry of reflection that will remind many readers of William Wordsworth. Brosman's poetry is by turns cosmopolitan, tasting of a broad range of places and landscapes, and steeped in the American South and Southwest, where she has lived most of her life. What makes such poems a pleasure to read is the way they invite one into the entire world, not just wide of breadth but also rich in depth. I remain convinced Brosman's greatest strength is in a thematically and formally expansive poetry that sweeps us up into the life of her thought.

—from a review by James Matthew Wilson,
poetry editor of *Modern Age* and director
of the MFA program in Creative Writing,
University of St. Thomas

Poetry by Catharine Savage Brosman

Watering (Athens: University of Georgia Press, 1972)

Abiding Winter (Florence, Ky: R. L. Barth, 1983)

Journeying from Canyon de Chelly (Baton Rouge: Louisiana State University Press, 1990)

Passages (Baton Rouge: Louisiana State University Press, 1996)

The Swimmer and Other Poems (Edgewood, Ky: R.L. Barth, 2000)

Places in Mind (Baton Rouge: Louisiana State University Press, 2000)

Petroglyphs: Poems and Prose (Thibodaux: Jubilee, A Festival of the Arts, Nicholls State University, 2003)

The Muscled Truce (Baton Rouge: Louisiana State University Press, 2003)

Range of Light (Baton Rouge: Louisiana State University Press, 2007)

Breakwater (Macon: Mercer University Press, 2009)

Trees in a Park (Thibodaux: Chicory Bloom Press, 2010)

Under the Pergola (Baton Rouge: Louisiana State University Press, 2011)

On the North Slope (Macon: Mercer University Press, 2012)

On the Old Plaza (Macon: Mercer University Press, 2014)

A Memory of Manaus (Macon: Mercer University Press, 2017)

Chained Tree, Chained Owls: Quintains (Columbia: Green Altar / Shotwell Publishing, 2020)

Clara's Bees (Omaha: Little Gidding Press, 2021)

Arm in Arm

Poems

Catharine Savage Brosman

MERCER UNIVERSITY PRESS
Macon, Georgia

MUP/ /P639

© 2022 by Mercer University Press
Published by Mercer University Press
1501 Mercer University Drive
Macon, Georgia 31207

25 24 23 22 21   5 4 3 2 1

Books published by Mercer University Press are printed on acid-free paper
that meets the requirements of the American National Standard for
Information Sciences—Permanence of Paper for Printed Library Materials.

Printed and bound in the United States.

This book is set in Adobe Caslon Pro.

Cover/jacket design by Burt&Burt.

ISBN   978-0-88146-831-1
Cataloging-in-Publication Data is available from the Library of Congress

To Kate, Brian, Clara, and Julian Deimling,
and in memory of my parents
and Pat, "my great companion."

MERCER UNIVERSITY PRESS

Endowed by

TOM WATSON BROWN
and
THE WATSON-BROWN FOUNDATION, INC.

CONTENTS

Acknowledgments

The author is grateful to the Little Gidding Press for permission to reprint poems from *Clara's Bees* (2021) and to editors of the periodicals where the following poems first appeared:

Able Muse: "Chrysanthemums";

Academic Questions, published by the National Association of Scholars: "Aglaonema," "Bloody Marys," "A Call from Porlock," "Clara's Bees," "Dinant, August 1914," "For a Champion," "Heart," "A Note to One Deceased," "Pat Curating His Library," "The Wolves Are Out";

Alabama Literary Review: "Arm in Arm," "Normandy, 7 August 1944," "Romaine," "Tulips in a Vase";

Arkansas Review: A Journal of Delta Studies: "The Mimosa," "Old Mr. Chauvin," "Three Sonnets for Stella";

Christianity and Literature: "Saint Dorothy," "Saint Nicholas";

Chronicles: A Magazine of American Culture: "At Sea," "Contagion," "Kit Carson in the Navajo Lands," "Mackenzie in the Western Range";

First Things: "Saint Gertrude," "Saint Lucy," "Saint Vincent of Saragossa";

Louisiana Literature: A Review of Literature and the Humanities, Southeastern Louisiana University, Hammond, La.: "Mimosa," "Screen," "Submersible," "Yellow Mustang";

The Lyric: "Colorado, 1935," "Girls' Weekend," "Meyer Lemons";

Modern Age: "Charming the Beasts," "Jean Cassou in Prison," "Saint George and the Dragon," "Saint Peter Bestowing the Holy Spirit";

North American Anglican: "Blue Heron by the Pond," "Compiègne," "Saint John the Baptist";

POEM: "Two Weavings."

I.

Arm in Arm

—"I would give the whole world to walk around New York arm in arm with my mother." —S.Y.

Arms linked and shoulders touching, feet in rhythm,
faces lit by the delights of laughter, talk,
close harmony—what homages to love and friendship!
Once, Pat and I walked arm in arm,
along an aisle, new husband, wife, to happiness.
We strolled in Paris one sweet summer, too—
the very picture of romance. And near
his lifetime's end, we walked in London, shivering

(as it was January), both slightly lame (the shoe
that pinched me, Pat's bad knees), but celebrating
older love, the sort that won't give up.
My parents, earlier—I must not forget: the three of us
along canals in Amsterdam, and later
on a Paris boulevard. We stopped at an appealing
bistrot where Vivaldi's *Seasons* gave a voice
to time as passing, always—my mother wondering

at the customs: large dogs, quiet, orderly; two lovers
kissing, each with glass in hand, on a bench
below the mirrors, the quintessential image of *amour*,
reflected for us. Other threads of recollection:
friends from Catalonia—she British, born in Ceylon,
and he, a native Catalan, a novelist.
We met in London at a conference, walked arm
in arm through Gordon Square; then they invited me

to visit for a week their country house outside Olot.
Elsewhere, happy scenes of holding hands,
the way my grandson, not quite grown, gave his to me,
half-guiding, half-supporting me discreetly
past the semi-darkness of the entryway and down
the steps, hollowed and too steep, in Diocletian's Palace.
What comes to mind most dearly are Pat's hands,
when he was old—strong, sensitive, with wrists still

powerful from slamming tennis shots—and that day
when on a tourist train he held my own
so tenderly that others in the coach inquired how long
we'd been married. Two answers, there. Another
moment: Michelangelo, the Sistine Chapel.
Now I imagine copper clouds at sunset, Pat appearing
as they part, reaching downward to me, arm
extended—smiling, signaling, his fingers touching mine.

Romaine

It's labeled "artisan"—a current word
seducing buyers prone to snobbery,
whence higher price. (Still, have we ever heard
of workshop turnips, studio broccoli?)

But this time it makes sense. Each head, "petite,"
is tender, outer leaves curled back a bit
and flounced, the rest, like tiny rowboats, neat,
concentric, nested, to great benefit.

For, wrapped around themselves, by nature's art,
they are untouched by anything—pristine,
protecting, as a lover might his heart,
their subtle prism, half-earthy, half-marine.

With care I peel away three leaves, no, four,
arrange them cunningly—an amulet—
slice cucumber, tomatoes ("heirloom"), pour
a "cold-pressed" oil- and red-wine vinaigrette.

Voilà! I yield to vegetable guile,
in short—and marketers. It's justified;
they nourish us with taste, in leafy style.
A mineral world and I must have our pride.

Mackenzie in the Western Range

—For Martha Mackenzie

I am a Scotsman, not demonstrative,
though not quite dour. Determined, rather—firm
and quiet. I was born to hardy Gaels,
on Lewis, in the Outer Hebrides,
with deep traditions. When my mother died
my father took me to New York to join
my uncle John. That was two years before
the war. Both Loyalists, they fought, but feared

for me, and sent me off to Montreal.
Apprenticed to a merchant, I remained,
and thus was there in eighty-seven when
his company became North West. To deal
in furs, one must outwit the Hudson Bay
monopoly, or find new sources. That
explains an enterprise, ill-organized:
Lake Athabasca to Slave Lake, thence west-

ward, as was thought, to reach a bay or arm
of the Pacific and establish routes
and posts for trapping, trade. Instead, we found
the "Disappointment River," leading north
to Arctic seas. —A wiser man, I worked
one year with sextant, stars, and then sailed back
to Scotland to be trained in longitudes,
before another effort—this time, though,

with guides (two Indians, skeptical), six French
Canadians, and my lieutenant, so to speak,
McKay. Ourselves, our arms, provisions, goods
as gifts encumbered the canoe—all told,
two tons. Our food was pemmican, the most
efficient nourishment, or, when at hand,
fresh game, fowl, fish. Our waterway, the Peace,
the only river *through* the Rockies, flows

northeast; ascending, we might cross and meet
a westward drainage. It was springtime—May;
long days grew longer: we arose at four.
The woods and meadows shone, exuberant.
But small impediments and losses count
when multiplied: a compass, gone; leaks, rips
in the canoe; defections; delicate
rapports with natives; shortly, lashing winds,

rough waters. Then cold rain, a freeze. We heard
no craft could ride the upper rapids, pinched
between steep walls; below them, currents raged.
And portages!—chevaux de frise, they were,
almost impassible for us, with loads
too heavy, falling from fatigue. Or else
we towed the pirogue by the river edge
in shallows, for long miles, or, numb from cold

and ice, bent over, pushed. Why do free men
choose risk, distress? Since rest will come at last,
with age or death, why not prefer it now,
I asked myself, my shoes worn out, feet cracked
and bleeding. Every day, though, we began
again—the boulders, défilés, the climbs,
descents. Discovery alone could not
suffice—discovery of *lands*, I mean.

>

The suffering is the coin. It was mid-June
by then. Once past the Great Divide, deterred
by talk of danger down a major stream,
we struck off overland, by portages
and sundry burns. Some rum remained, a boon.
At last, the coast. Thank God!—a continent
traversed, the sparkling shield of water, spears
of sun, sea spume. Such honors. It was well.

Tulips in a Vase

They know that they are beautiful. They turn
to show their profile, bend a willowy stem,
adjust their mien (one redhead seems to burn
with languorous henna streaks). Each stratagem

is clever, catching eye and thought. And we
respond indulgently with care and praise:
fresh water, stimulants, the eager fee
for beauty. One, pale pink, attempts to raise

her languid petals, parting at the throat,
while two, sun-yellow, shyly hold a pose
of modesty. Such tactics may denote
an ingénue who shuns the blowsy rose

and innocently keeps *le naturel*;
or can they be, perhaps, some artifice
learned even in the tulip fields, learned well?
Their coquetry is sui generis

at least. And ours? It's ancient—budding girls,
old divas, all the same—instinctive, cool,
directed toward the flattery, flowers, pearls
that prove how far each sex can play the fool.

Clara's Bees

i

The back garden is arranged for them—path cleared,
a stand assembled for the hive, fresh plantings,
friendly, flourishing. When the bees will come, though,
is uncertain. They were ordered months ago,
for Easter Week, from Italy! They will be driven,
I assume, by the *Servizio postale* from the *campagna*
to some *ufficio* in the city, thence an airport,
flown across the ocean to New York, then find

themselves—to their surprise?—in Bedford-Stuyvesant.
How adaptable are they? Oh, quite, I think.
Moreover, they are guaranteed—by Ebay! Fancy that.
Apis mellifera: a honeyed name. This past season
during long hours of darkness they slept in, Circadian
like us; being shut up a while for shipping
should not damage them. But the times are bad—
the year of pestilence. Italy is devastated, New York,

worse. Will the plane take off? And can it be *essential*
these days to deliver honeybees? Meanwhile,
Clara has, to occupy her time and thoughts,
her ancient Greek and French, her history, English,
physics, math, and chemistry. We are in suspense,
imagining the garden shortly, all abuzz. What a refuge!
—like the fragrant villa outside Florence
where Boccaccio and his friends escaped the plague.

Foretelling mellic words, bees swarmed to land
on tiny Plato's lips as he lay slumbering in his cradle.
Thenceforth he favored them, in fact,
in metaphor: they were the souls of dead philosophers
perhaps, returned, or represented virtues—
both alike and different. Yet with a warning: dulcitude,
said Socrates, is toxic, dangerous to moderation. Oh,
Clara, shining sweetness does befit you,

but, too, the golden mean of thought.—The bees
have landed, stirring from their drowse a bit, sending
scouts, it would appear, to find the nectar
in the marigolds, and waiting, we suppose, for warmer
weather, while the queen stays in her traveling cage
before her sortie to lay eggs. Her troops
are numerous—ten thousand, so it's said. Imagine!
Think of future vectors on display—authentic

bee-lines, but with variations, deviations, multiplying
as the little darlings flit from flower to flower—
pollen ready, juices nectarous—in all directions,
to their purpose. It's ballet, but modern
in its choreography. Like Clara, also poised to venture,
all intent, the very image of a body's rationale:
to be, and be one's possibilities—the muscles flexing
toward the goal, the pulse of datum turning to idea.

Heart

—In memory of F. K. H.

For years, her valves inflamed, she lay abed—
rheumatic fever. Games and playmates, banned;
no school; just lessons at her mother's hand.
At times, she must have wished that she were dead.

There was no treatment then, no hope of cure,
save *rest*. What irony: a *child*'s disease,
already noted by Hippocrates.
What recourse had she but endure, endure?

She grew somehow, and managed to excel
in several ways, despite a damaged lung.
Her resolutions: always to stay young;
at work, in love, in friendship, do it well.

Above all, play. She gave it her whole heart.
For seven years she'd thought of it as art.

Grace King on the Bayous, 1862

Not yet ten years of age—already wise,
however, in the ways of war—she fled
New Orleans with her family to escape
the Federals. Her father, warned in time
(he would not take the Union oath), had quit
his office casually, but half-disguised,
and headed west, toward New Iberia,
behind the lines, where he owned land. He sent

brief word that they should join him there. The house
was seized that very day, their goods destroyed,
or carried to the street for plundering.
The world had given way. To leave was quite
forbidden, though. Some poor connection, now
of high estate, procured for them a pass;
but it must have a countersignature.
All wit, composure, purpose, Mrs. King

went out to face "Beast" Butler in his lair.
To no avail; he was not moved. By chance,
another general, outside the door,
had heard, and signed. She found a steamboat (Grace
could not say how) to take them—mother, babe
in arms, the Presbyterian *Grandmamma*,
the children, servants—up the River. Not
the Ark; but safety. As they said goodbye

beneath the fragrant jasmine, neighbors thrust
at Grace an old rag doll, quite artless. —First,
a levee landing, by the stubbled cane.
A deck hand rolled a flour barrel down
the plank. "Not mine," said Mrs. King. "Hush, hush,"
the captain warned; "I'm a Confederate."
At two plantations, there was help; a cart
conveyed them farther on. They slept

in comfort, once. A ferry was half-burnt;
yet they engaged the dubious owner, reached
le Bayou Plaquemine, went on by barge
along another, heartened, then two lakes
by skiff. A sandbar pinioned them; night fell.
In silence, *Grandmamma* appealed to God.
How many days had passed? How many ways
had Providence assisted them? Her faith

was firm. Marooned, for hours each one hallooed—
in vain. Again by chance, the father, at an inn
(not far, miraculously), overheard
a band of soldiers, dressed in gray, relate
how they had stopped a woman on a lake,
surrounded by her family, questioned her.
It could have been his wife! "Such charm, her way
of speaking! And the girl—how droll!" He cut

on horseback through a swamp, got help, then rode
beside the shore and commandeered a boat,
and men to go ahead with lights. At last,
faint shouts, a choking voice replying, sounds
of oar-locks grating—blest deliverance.
Such cries, such gratitude! And such a find:
concealed deep in the flour were medicines,
addressed to troops nearby; the ragged doll,

its seams undone, revealed a wad of bills.
Unconscious contraband! The servants, freed,
remained with them throughout the war, and most
returned. Grace never would forget. For what
the whirlwind left in the debris was love,
resolve, new sympathies, and her great gift:
a girl's, a woman's words, as witnesses,
the shiny coins of patience and the mind.

On Poetry

It's no mere decoration; it is *art*.
Like music, bound to breathing, though beyond,
it's feeling turned to sound—a *meta*-part
of being bodied, a magician's wand.

So versatile! Shoot off a verse, a dart—
the mode of Swift and Pope; few may respond
in kind, but they'll remember it. Or start
a conversation! Smiling, wave a frond

of airy nothings at a party; please
the guests; astonish them, perhaps! A name,
a title: they'll recall a line with ease

or even quote a sonnet. Some may claim
a poet sister, cite themselves! Conceal
impatience; sacrifice to the ideal.

Images

—After Debussy

"Reflets d'eau"

A pond so quiet nothing stirs—glaze, reflections.
Clouds appear in shades of black
and white; sculpted trees, still, almost mannerist,
and leafy clusters, like acanthus, hold their being.
Sultry air weighs upon the surface; nothing
rises to disturb it save small bubbles, as a turtle
breathes discreetly. Modest rings of ripples—notes
barely audible—last a moment only. Suddenly,

a wind from nowhere skips across the water, waking
it, inviting it to movement, and the sunlight,
willing, multiplies on wavelets, brilliant, high-
toned, running everywhere, and all at once,
with a bass below in darker notes. Plane impressions
gather texture, depth, and yield to Cubist imitations;
clouds ruffle, contrasts magnify
in modern chords and disaccords; then calm again.

"Poissons d'or"

Startled, they appear like grace notes chasing
others, fluid color flashing within silvered water—
streams of lambent ovals, wholes, eddying, which split,
then coalesce in chords, to part again, exploding,
by quick centrifugal acceleration. Their luminescence
flares, scarlet, gold, bright orange, wheeling
through the patchy light among dead leaves
and fallen flowers of Rosa de Montana vine. Bred

to beauty, to give images of wealth, to please a lover,
entertain, impress a guest, they're riches
for the eye. A rustling wind picks up the motion
in its own sonorities, playing in the trees, teasing,
crumpling the shiny skin of shadowed water.
What can that be to these golden sprites,
running on, tumbling, taking along the music
of the day until it edges downward, falls into the night?

Two Weavings

Called rugs, or carpets, genuine Navajo,
my two are small, not practical for feet;
instead, they're made for decoration, show—
southwestern signs of riches, but discreet.

With nubby surface, whip-stitched ends, black, gray,
they both proclaim their origin, their land—
the sandy waste that stretches far away,
the mesas, lightning, rain, the maker's hand.

For each is personal. Here's Nellie John—
a photo, with her rug, her guarantee—
her weathered face, her gaze a paragon
of polished art and authenticity.

Her weaving's from the workshop "Two Gray Hills,"
its wools undyed, as carded from the sheep—
brown, beige, gray, cream—made drama by her skills.
The other's striking beauty lies in deep

carnelian red, a powerful design
suggesting arrows, birds, electric storm,
the blood-stained sun and sacrificial wine,
great spirits manifest in desert form.

Old Mr. Chauvin

When Old Mr. Chauvin sat outside in summer,
in Louisiana heat, he wore a cardigan
of heavy wool, a woody green. It matched the foliage
around him—banana trees, bamboo, cat's paw,
huge oaks that overhung the fences.
Only think: the temperatures, when "cool,"
were in the eighties; ninety-five perhaps when "warm."
Humidity nearly as high, of course, blown

in one's face (or, on lazy days, just wafted idly)
from the river, many lakes, and Gulf, some distance
off but not too far for wind. He was
a widower who'd come from Terrebonne Parish
to New Orleans so his daughter
could take care of him. He didn't much like
air conditioning—the noise, the draft along his neck;
he knew it was unnatural. After all,

he hadn't had it as a boy way down on Bayou Black,
and he'd survived. So, in the afternoon,
following "dinner" and a necessary nap, he makes
his way with care down four back steps,
his sweater on, to get warmed up
in nature. He listens to cicadas, traffic (panel trucks
and cars, not airboats, graceful pirogues),
shouting from the neighbors, the blind man

two fences down finding his way back
to his garage abode and cursing. Old Mr. Chauvin
has seen and heard a lot. The bayou
is a little slice of life, provincial surely,
but as true as one could wish: no need to see a wider
world—not Paris (anyway, his ancestors
were Bretons, coastal people, fishermen,
and fiercely independent), not Chicago or New York—

the names, the thought appall him. True, that Guidry
boy named Ron, from Lafayette (he'd known
a lot of Guidrys), the famous pitcher,
was a New York Yankee—but he'd had the sense
to come back home when he retired.
And Bobby Hébert settled in New Orleans. —Oh,
his daughter's calling—him? her husband?
She comes out, for no good reason but that she, too,

likes the sultry heat, the shade below the oak trees,
the flowering Rosa de Montana vine
and bougainvillea, deep pink; she too remembers
Bayou Black. When he is gone, and she
must wear a sweater in the summer,
she'll sit out and think of him, at peace with her life,
knowing how she might have said things to him better,
but turning into him, or wishing she could.

Blue Heron by the Pond

With sunlight on his plumage, noble stance,
he's fully grown, a handsome specimen,
ideally formed, by some design or chance—
exemplar of the avian citizen.

He's quite alone; he wants no company.
Immobile, his attention occupied
by possibilities I cannot see
below, he rules the grassy berm—with pride,

you'd say. For him, the pond's a rippling prize,
well stocked with turtles, minnows, larger fish,
green water weeds and sheer-winged dragonflies—
and safe, fulfilling every angler's wish.

His stillness interrupts the human day,
its moods, emotions, motives, what will come,
or came before, and all that flows away.
(It's strange how emptiness can be the sum

of so much tumult.) Suddenly, the spear
has struck; his gullet twists, until the small
commotion ends. An image, now austere
again, endures; no further sign at all.

His day will pass thus, standing, stalking, brain
and eye on duty constantly, alert
yet unreflecting, destined to remain
objective, while we love, regret, and hurt.

Weyer's Cave

Careful, for the steps here
descend like memory; we do not know
how far we may fall,
looking for telluric fire
in the dark. Steady as breath,
cool water drips below
onto time turned stone,

connecting the extremes
of space, as though in desire.
Now through a kaleidoscope we move
past pendulous leaves,
heavier than dreams,
and cross immemorial groves of fern
where a figure grieves,

Eurydice in tears.
Our footfalls echo small.
While we can still return,
lead me back to sheaves
of light; I shall go down alone
this way later, bridging through love
the shaded stream of death.

Logan, As We Said…

—In memory of P. J. T.

For Logan, as we said, is handsome, sleek,
with tiger stripes of mottled gray and black,
his character ideal. But Time must wreak
its malice, finding hidden ways to wrack

a furry body. Logan, as we said,
excels—long whiskers and keen ears, eyes hewn
of gems and liquid coal, good carriage. Bred
in Baton Rouge, his mother a Maine Coon,

his sire of unknown race. A lucky cat,
dear Logan lived, while passed from hand to hand.
Despite the blot, he's an aristocrat,
we've said. As undervalued contraband,

he got somehow to Texas, where, by chance,
he found a caring biped—what a friend!—
all falling into place by happenstance.
Dear Logan is a lovely cat and can't offend

a soul, as we have said; and sometimes fate
does intervene, to further happiness.
But now, he's ill, his being in the strait
of death from inner failures. We profess

to understand, but we get just the face
of things, the words, no more. For, prince or waif
—and Logan, we have said, has had the grace
of both—we must be mortal; none is safe.

23

Trees

—For M. and C.

i

We're at the table in the kitchen nook,
my hosts and I, one evening. Suddenly,
a boom, a crack, a crash. We run to look,
a window first, a door. Too dark to see

much. But the sound came, surely, from the street.
Two steps, a gate; we're out. In feeble glow,
a formless shadow, lying near our feet
—a phantom tangle—waves, as if to show

good will. A fallen pine tree? Just a limb—
enormous, though, wounds visible, the pith,
pale sinews, torn. The spectacle is grim:
a part "untimely ripped"—old Pelops' myth,

his shoulder gone. Leaves, branches, twigs are strewn
about, from trauma. Ah, a lantern! There,
azalea banks are split; the lawn looks hewn
as if maliciously; a small parterre

is ruined. Retrospectively, we fear
what might have happened: man and dog, out late,
or cyclist, crushed. All life's a strange career.
Fraternal thoughts accompany our fate.

ii

Camping one summer, in the San Juans, we cousins slept,
cooked, ate beneath a heavy canopy of spruce—
great Englemanns—and Douglas fir, with branches layered
thickly, latticing. Deep beds of needles underfoot,
cracking, aged, powdery, softened our steps, our bodies'
rest. Late rain fell every afternoon, adding
to the conifers' perfume its musky petrichor; but only
scattered drops could reach us, sheltered in our arbor, dry,
as we collected kindling, pulled up chairs, poured our wine.

iii

Sometimes I think I love trees the way one loves
one's own body, so familiar, yet so strange,
born, grown despite us, with its own rationale; dying also.
Aren't we walking trees, head in the clouds, reaching
for light, for space, limbs extended to embrace the world,
trunk rooted, not to earth, though, but our past;
always trailing, too, connections with our fellows,
the way conifers weave their branches, making dark wattles,
the way aspen are wired among others underground?

Fourteen Modern Poems in the Chinese Manner

1. Little Tree

The little tree was moving rapidly, borne up,
half-wrapped, in a clay pot by a strong man.
How rare to see a tree in someone's hand!
And passing through a hallway in a high-rise,
heading outside! To see the sky, perhaps,

the wispy clouds, just bits of dream, or those
that flow in thought, or massive thunderheads,
round islands rising. Might they grant a favor,
darken, let drops fall on eager leaves, delight
the roots with soft rain running down the soul?

2. Mimosa

A low wall runs beside a pond, under trees.
In a crack, a bit of green, the tiniest of plants—
two pennate leaves, compound, no bigger
than a fingernail. The tree, entire, is there,
its future, past, its DNA. The striving world

is just a mass of molecules, never lost, merely
elided, metamorphosed. —Oh, here comes
a friend! The wind won't blow our words
away; they'll drift a moment, by the water;
we'll write them in the book of passing hours.

3. Submersible

Li Po and NASA reached out to the moon,
such shiny dust. No luster on the ocean floor
—a black abyss; no fish for an imaginary
line—just primordial lumps of cells. Still,
one Vescovo plunged in a titanium submersible

of his design, to study depths of nothingness.
The engineer, albeit fearful, did accompany
him, lending faith. I sit here by the bayou,
watching the flow, glimpsing shadows: gar
and catfish. The moon has risen, golden eye.

4. A Poet

My friend the Chinese scholar translates,
lectures, comments, and composes his own
poetry—and does the marketing for two
on Saturdays. As regular as tides. There
he is, in a photo, holding a glass of bourbon,

honey-hued. He sends me poems rhyming
"moon," "Sassoon" and "queen," "serene."
All poets labor, sowing syllables and reaping
verses. *His* catch memories in a net. Here,
a toast to words, the spirit's food, and beauty.

5. Screen

—For J. C.

It fills an ample opening between two rooms,
so that always one is both within, without,
facing one scene, then another, golden, or black
lacquer—thoughts on a cusp. Water undulates
and ripples, bright with sun; moss dangles down

from trees; a bluebird flashes; and two egrets
wait to strike. If I move, choose the dark reverse,
it's bamboo, leaves, webs, for revery, for regret.
I look out at the clouds lying low on the horizon—
or in water, mirrored each way. How do I know?

6. Solitude

The plague's still with us, brought by travelers
from the East. The isolation's difficult, death
worse yet, smelly and distressing. When will we
hear good news? But I should not complain;
since I lost my great companion, I've been solo

anyhow, with bits of music, poetry, old history
books, and friends' letters as good cheer. A new
tome brings delight, and, even more, familiar
works forgotten, now uncovered. To all, *salut*!
I shall pour myself tonight a *coupe* of pinot noir.

7. Journey

— *For C. L. M.*

My friend is leaving for Den Haag tomorrow—
too far. (Even in our time, it lies across the sea.)
I'll think of her and her new digs, set among
the North Sea dunes, canals, and tulip fields.
She'll bike, carry net shopping bags, cross hump-

back bridges, cook fine dinners for her husband.
At my throat now is an ornament she fashioned—
choker-style—ocean blue and silver. Tasteful,
of course. From time to time, she'll read a poem
of my composition; I shall put on azure stones.

8. Dream

My friend's in Brussels now, enclosed by mist,
along with new miasmas of the pestilence. Few
ways to form acquaintances; half-empty streets,
shops shuttered, cold cafés. Two local tongues
compete, not kindly. Yet she goes out, carries

her *filet*, stops at the greengrocer's, butcher's,
vintner's, chooses Belgian chocolates, smiles
at everyone, as if enjoying still a sunlit dream—
the sand, rocks, funny cactus, vast blue skies
of that far, foreign land where she left memories.

9. Red Bird

A scroll by Hua Yan depicts a long-tailed bird
of scarlet on a bamboo branch. —For years,
a bit of art, a bird constructed of real feathers,
matted, framed, observed me from a shelf. Red
flashes out from cardinals in our crepe myrtles,

brilliant in the sunlight, warbling gloriously.
They shine among the riches of the day. Now,
I'll hear their music in my head, since night
has fallen. Having flown, the feathered image
sings in Brooklyn, in the house of those I love.

10. In a Garden

Since death visited, my British friend has lived
as she can—bungalow, furnished conservatory,
the temperamental sun. She has no special
shrine; most of his books were sold. The piano
resonates, though; she sings for memory's sake.

And there's a garden, tended well, as if by him.
We stroll the pavers among allium, geraniums,
and poppies, watch fat pigeons at the bird bath.
Where is that other life? The wind stirs up
the birch and shows the pale underside of things.

11. Sunset

Various small *objets* from Asia strike my eye
as I turn on a lamp by the piano. They exist
to little purpose, but to *be* and please. For what
use, then, is a consciousness? Here's a warrior,
bronze, from Burma, I believe, but his weapon

has been broken off. In a tarnished silver set
(torii and pagoda), the finial is missing, though
in my mind, they're perfect, like the ivory fan,
the enameled elephant. A final glint of sunset
passes. Clouds blow in, darkly. I imagine stars.

12. Pronghorns

—For R. and S.

In camouflage—striped tones of earth and straw—
they move almost invisibly along the winter range,
foraging barrenness. I watch them graze, distanced
or in clusters, following what vectors? The wind
whirrs. One lifts its head, looks my way, painted

luminously. "Come," say my friends, "let's leave
now for the winery." Oh, soon we also shall enjoy
spare morsels of the desert. My scattered thoughts
collect, ruminate a moment with the pronghorns,
then fly off toward the mountains, serrated, blue.

13. By Fountain Creek

—Cascade, Colorado, 2016

Below the terrace where we lunch, a narrow
streamlet, shallow, too, rippling barely above
the stones. It dips, though, fast, falling noisily,
gurgling its water music for the pines, for us.
Long-needled tresses wave as if in greeting,

green to bright sky-blue: "I'm here!" And so
are we now, happily. The snow's still melting,
though, along the peak, and flooding is implicit.
Wisely, I have filled my ears with silver tones,
my lungs with mountain air, my eyes with leaves.

14. Looking at Pike's Peak

—Colorado Springs, 2019

The silver maple rests a graceful limb along
the railing of the balcony. Sparrows often
come to visit, watching, twittering, fluttering,
flying off. What hours we spent there, he
and I, from breakfast on to dusk, and nights

of crowded stars. We heard the bells at noon
and vespers, watched the shadow commandeer
the mountain, the maple lose its leaves in fall.
Such loss in my heart now, since I must say
farewell. The peak takes on late amber glow.

II.

Grace King Abroad

She'd published a novella, to acclaim,
and shorter fiction; she had earned a place
in letters. Yet conventional; no blame
attached to her, no feminist disgrace.

To write was, in her circles, honored; she
was gifted and determined. Talent paid.
She made acquaintances, worked tirelessly,
went north, found publishers, and stayed

some while, a charming southern guest, the toast
of many gatherings. New Orleans looks
to Europe, not New England, though. The ghost
of great French authors lingered in her books.

The Continent! Her family had no wealth,
however—vanished in the war; too many girls,
a drunken brother, and her father's health
destroyed; her manuscripts, her only pearls.

She pinched, and saved, and wrote and wrote,
and got a gift or so. From somewhere east—
New York or Boston—she would take a boat,
alone, or with her sister Nan; the least

of ships would do. Although *The Century*
paid well, and *Harper's* better, she must wait
so long for checks! Her brother finally
sent funds he'd promised. It was not too late.

The wherewithal in banks, she left, with Nan.
High time, she thought, for her for visit France,
her literary home. Abroad, her plan
was thrifty, but ambitious, for the chance

might not recur. So, Ireland, Liverpool
and Cambridge, London, briefly, then across
the Channel. Paris was, for her, the school
of culture, where no day could be a loss—

salons, museums, lectures, bookstores, art
in galleries, the streets, and in the air.
Too close, the sisters quarreled, though; Grace's heart
was pulled by ills at home, by pockets bare,

despite economy. A treasured friend,
Olivia, the wife of one Mark Twain,
invited them to Italy to spend
a month in Florence. Each would entertain

the rest. A daughter played; the great man read
aloud from Browning; they took drives;
they lingered, talking, laughing, before bed.
It was, Grace wrote, the "cream" of travel—lives

connected fruitfully, hard, glittering gem
of memory. (The filth, the "one-horse creek"—
the Arno—did not matter: to condemn
the city would devalue the antique,

the friends.) Their fortunes failed thereafter. Grace,
though able to return to Paris, lost
old friends and mother, while the chase
for money never ended and the cost

grew greater on her mind. Sam Clemens filed
for bankruptcy. Then illness, death. Could each
remember Florence, and be reconciled
to having happiness beyond their reach?

News!

(An Epithalamium)

Just listen to this news. A man named Ray
retired yesterday, still young, and sound
of mind (his choice of bride attests). Today,
he will be married on French Lake, around

this morning hour, in Massachusetts. Then
a wedding breakfast. In the afternoon,
much packing going on, two houses. When
they've had enough, a fancy dinner—moon

above a terrace, with gastronomy,
champagne, and music. Movers will arrive
before they know it. What commotion, glee,
impatience—all without regrets. They'll drive,

cross-country, as the latest pioneers,
to Arizona and their new abode—
adobe, ranch-style, with fine views. The years
will validate their pick in mates, their mode

of being, shaped by cactus, desert trees,
dry mountains, rocks—each a conservator,
pursuing happiness, the other's ease,
economies of rain, a metaphor

for life. So celebrate with me this time,
and mark your calendar in sandstone red
with roses, hearts, and stars—a paradigm
of settled love, as Ray and Sarah wed.

Cedar Waxwings

Like us, they're masked, with lighted crest,
but sociable—no "distancing" required.
They move in umber clouds, as if possessed
by poets' frenzy, suddenly inspired.

So here, shot from the blue, they come—a curve
above the treetops, an elastic band
that suddenly contracts, then, in a swerve,
a brushstroke, a *piqué*, descends, to land

among the Yaupon holly limbs. They feast
on scarlet berries, swallowing them whole,
susurrant, scavenging as if the least
were good. —A subtle sign, a caracole,

and they are on the wing again, to storm
a farther tree, the season's rich reward,
then, having banqueted, collect and form
a well-fed flock to glorify the Lord.

The Dentist's Chair

Two dentists in one afternoon! I'm whipped,
but must drive home, disoriented, sore.
No appetite; my poet's wings are clipped.
The day is nearly gone. Besides, there's more.

I've got a notable anomaly
along one side. No danger; little pain;
displeasure, though, in curvature. For me
no "easy" seating. "Straight!" is my refrain,

or flat in bed. The dentist's chair is bent.
When I have spent some while—an hour or so—
acutely angled, I'm contorted, rent,
with ribs pushed out of place (they even show)

and terrible discomfort. Which is worse—
the drilling noise, dry mouth, a bitter taste
from antiseptic, scrapers, picks, the curse
of hurting in the good teeth, too (a waste

of bodily defenses)—or the sense
my side will split, not laughing? Now, *le stress*
has given me a foot cramp. Very tense,
I am, and low on calories—a mess.

The dentist's capable, experienced, nice.
Assuring me it's "nearly in the bag,"
she adds I must return, not once, but twice!
The thought, the awful taste—I almost gag.

In other words, she's getting "to the root
of things." Indeed, down to the very nerve.
What choice have I? *My* misery is moot.
My teeth are trumps; they'll get what they deserve.

>

More scratching, poking, digging, pulling. Will
she use the drill again? I cringe. "At last,"
she says, "it's done, for now." I'm grateful. Still…
The final flourish is a water-blast.

Appointments must be made. "Yes, I can come
next week." If I were someone else, I'd scream.
(Think Munch.) I say goodbye, half-witted, numb.
En route back home, I'll stop to get ice cream.

Conjecture

i

First, it was Goldbach's, or at least it bears his name,
as he proposed it in the eighteenth century:
"Every even positive integer is the sum of two primes."
A thought well demonstrated, we may say,
since it's been shown to hold for all such integers
up to 4 x 10^{18} —more than the number of seconds
since the formation of the earth. To hold, that is,
so far. Proven, no. What about figures on to infinity?

An ingenious proof, or one small counterexample, one,
would settle the whole matter in an instant. Why not
find one? —So that's what Pat was working on,
for years, staring into space, pencil, clipboard in hand,
or at night in bed to pacify the mental imps
that beset us all. His were conjectures on a conjecture,
working by trial and error, eliminating, narrowing
the lines of possibility. Somehow, a journalist

got wind of this work and his Quasicircles, which he'd
lectured on at Rice. So he was in the newspaper:
mass storage specialist at Shell, and paid
to think; tennis player on the weekends; gentleman rancher;
bitten by Goldbach's bug, at work on the improbable.
Then the problem moved into another mode:
in odd moments, at the piano, he sketched out "Conjecture,"
a short piece with a haunting quality. Doubtless

Goldbach would have liked surprising tonal contrasts
here and there, the final E♭ minor chord;
in travels around Europe, surely he heard Bach
and Telemann performed, Lully, Couperin.—A further
layer was devised and added when I came
along: I made of it an art song, musing on counterfactuals—
"If only!"—but it's moot and idle play, since,
as the past circled around, our end was our beginning.

ii

We know what could have been, yet was not, will not be.
It's only vacuous; to dream is just a game,
a mere conjecture, drawn from restless day's debris,
though when I think of time, I'm tempted all the same.
I muse on all the years we lost together,
suffering the heart's cold weather,
wondering anew then whether
fate
might let us someday meet again,
and when—
and you might love me still, though it was late.

The past is past; such speculation is a pose,
a gust of wind that combs the grass without a trace,
red petals crushed from an imaginary rose.
It's needless anyway; you're here now, in your place.
If life appears, alas, to be in tatters—
fallen leaves a rainstorm scatters—
suppositions aren't what matters;
no!
Love brought, intuitive and swift,
its gift,
resolving time's conundrums, as we show.

Contagion

—November 2020

We've got four elevators, one for freight.
For forty floors, you'd think they would suffice;
we residents would not be forced to wait
inordinately. That assumption's nice,

but wrong. Today I tried to go downstairs
to mail three letters. I had on a mask.
Cars came; doors opened, briefly. No one shares
a ride, however; you can't even ask

without offense, for we're compelled, by rule,
to isolate ourselves. It's the disease,
of course—and our docility, a tool
for those in office. Smile as it may please

you, nothing's to be done; again, doors closed.
Ten elevators stopped. A doggie wagged
his tail at me; that's all. When I'd supposed
I must give up, an empty one! I bagged

it. Farther down, I let two people in.
In me, autonomy, and sense, run deep.
To others, judging for oneself is sin.
(Lord Fauci shakes his stick at us.) They're sheep—

a flock enfeebled by anxiety,
who will believe most any pseudo-fact
of "experts," even contradictory,
retracted soon, or plainly inexact.

>

Alighting, I encounter man and wife
attired like beekeepers. Who might they be?
Alone, molecular—that is not life
as we should wish it, reasonable, free.

The letters posted, I must stand in line
to ride upstairs. All right; that's not outrageous.
Reflect, though: power is not anodyne,
and tyranny, like Covid, is contagious.

For a Champion

I don't reply to insults often—not my style,
a waste of time. Besides, I was not reared
for such contentious intercourse. But while
I shall be reticent, a friend has cleared

my name—three missiles, launched in my defense!
King Arthur, were he here, with mighty sword,
would not be needed; courtesy, good sense,
poetic wit suffice. The fellow's gored.

He called my formal poems "precious," "prissy,"
ignoring women's nature, taste, and tone,
and treated me as just a worthless missy.
Had I been coarse, or "woke," I might have shone.

He thought it must have had to do with race,
or Tory prejudice (no alibi).
He's quite mistaken; that is not the case,
except in his strabismic, crooked eye.

He singled out a classical allusion,
as evidence of hopeless obsolescence.
I've read his stuff. Banal. To his confusion,
he'll see it all dissolve into putrescence.

So thank you, Sir, for taking up my cause,
my colors, Nature's hues, which he disdains.
Your mighty pen will surely get applause;
he'll get poetic justice for his pains.

The Wolves Are Out

A strange effect of this long quarantine:
the wolves are out. Like springtime, death, and war,
it leads men's latent fancies to convene
on love, or something like it. They explore

all avenues. One bluntly asked my name
as I passed by him at a musicale
outdoors; then, gesturing, said, "Your mother came
along, I see." But no!—coeval, *pal*

—both wrinkled women "of a certain age."
(Through vanity, I had on veiling, thus
disguising years.) Another personage—
a married man I know—made quite a fuss,

and mumbled "an affair…if I were free,"
then rearranged my shirt, *en décolleté*,
as though to guard my virtue! Just a *V*,
it was, though, in good taste and not *risqué*.

A third man shines by courtesy. No hook;
disinterested. I was in a café,
alone, a fork in one hand, and a book
beside me, open. Few were there that day.

I know the manager. "The bill, when you
are ready, please." "It's paid," he said. "But how?
You must be wrong." "That man who left, in blue,
took care of it." I understand; just now

I'd glimpsed a figure at the door. But why?
He did not ask my name, nor leave a card,
nor speak; just paid my check and his. I sigh.
The soul of tact. But don't let down your guard!

Tate Britain

— For J. W.—2019

i

All London's green and leafy in the sun,
day after day, this June. And we are here, a friend
and I, to see the city, from our old hotel
in Bloomsbury on Great Russell St., to distant sites,
the three-bus sort (no Underground for me—
new phobias). So Kensington one day, and Southwark
on another,.for a stroll, a meal, and Shakespeare.
Greenwich, too, an afternoon of walking,

climbing, taking in the picture. Now, we want to see
Tate Britain, Millbank, in Westminster. I know
it well. How can we reach it, though? A concierge
reassures us on directions and a bus or so. We're game;
let's go! The rides are lovely: much
of London's visible, the people (shoppers, students,
tourists looking lost); the Thames, its bridges; churches,
shops and houses, trees. We catch the second

bus. Riparian views, as I remember. We're obliged
to transfer once again. I cannot reconstruct the route.
All I recall is that the driver stopped and said,
"You'd better get off here, m' Luv—I won't
get any closer," adding, "Just a bit of walking; carry on."
By now, though, it is one o'clock, or past,
and Messer Gaster's calling. Nothing! No café
or restaurant, except a handsome place, faux-Tudor,

closed. Not yet near Pimlico, where I got off
the tube, in younger days. Oh, finally, here's a pub
that's open, though it's nearly two. Lunch
and wine are good, the hosts most pleasant. Art is still
ahead. We pass Ponsonby Terrace, of excellent
design; for a mere two million pounds, perhaps
a little less, I'd have myself a handsome London seat;
the Tate would be my neighbor and my muse.

ii

We've got to see the Blake collections, first—
past description in their genius. Then our errant ways
divert us, taking us by works of Henry Moore,
and we drop in on Lucian Freud, "The Girl
with a White Dog" and such. They're strong, I must
admit. But what we've come especially to see
are Turners—worth each step (we got quite weary
traveling, as it seemed, to the ends of London,

with sharp, enfeebling hunger). Oh, those Turner skies
and waters, merging in their moist perfection,
satisfying thought, matching desire! We pass
the gift shop, but I must go on; I'll come back later.
We reach the Turner rooms, eventually
all nine. Are some pieces new to me, rehung
or redisplayed; or have I just forgotten? Sketches,
drafts, unfinished canvasses are out, among the famous

works. We do each wall. Suddenly, I gasp: what's that
over my shoulder? Oh! "Moonlight, Millbank,"
done when Turner was just twenty-two. What genius!
Distant trees, the water lit, a sail, a church, and, low above
the murky riverscape, the moon—aglow, less aureate
than white. Another scene, at twilight—Harlech Castle,
on the bay of Cardigan—shows pale Atlantic lucence,
calm, and ships that ply it. Next, "The Flood,"

then landscapes with their brooks and aqueducts,
horned cattle, washerwomen, towering trees;
more harbors, scenes of Holland, Venice—
and a snowstorm Turner saw in Wales, all white.
They make me want to go there, live the wind, the waves,
the promise of departure, know the black-troughed
fear. Or stand along the Grand Canal, to paint
Palladian façades in shimmering sunlight, plumb the blue.

Bloody Marys

—For W. D. C.

Behold, the [sic] Hotel Belle View Royale—
a case of adding French to make a name
(half-right) sound elegant and not banal.
In time, the place may thereby earn acclaim.

Though situated on a lovely bay,
with splendid views, in Aberystwyth, Wales
(reason the more, perhaps, to add cachet?),
its mirrors, polished bar, and famous ales

are known to few. The town is small, remote;
the students at the *uni* cannot pay
for fancy wines and five-star *table d'hôte*.
There's very little custom on this day.

We choose two stools. The barman comes to take
our order. David smiles: "A Bloody Mary."
A puzzled silence, first ("How *does* one make
it?"—so we read the fellow's mind.) A query:

"What *is* it?" A tutorial ensues:
tall glasses, spirits, ice, *tomahto* juice,
Tabasco, Worcestershire ("Oh, this is news!"),
black pepper, celery. To introduce

a Welshman to the drink is a delight.
There's no Tabasco, though, not green, not red,
nor celery. "Those Spanish olives might
do nicely, or a pickled bean, instead."

The fellow comes around; he does his best.
We raise a glass to him, to Cymru pride.
We chatter, drink, and gaze out to the west,
where sunset spreads its silver on the tide,

and, with the barman, speak of New *Orleens*.
For us, a local dinner then, Welsh rabbit.
With or without Tabasco and green beans,
for him, a Bloody Mary's now a habit.

Annapurna

i

To tackle the Himalayas with skills
acquired on Mont Blanc and lower Alps
was risky, but our chance must not be lost.
Plans carefully laid out, developed, well
adjusted to the party and the task,
bode favorably, with experienced men,
support from France as needed, and resolve.
Mont Blanc is not five thousand meters high,

however—Annapurna, eight, and set
in an immense massif, unknown, complex,
imposing. Timing was not good, but how
could it have been, between the worst of cold
and June monsoons? False starts impeded us.
We changed directions, cut new routes across
the mountain mazes, crevasses, couloirs,
with mute or enigmatic maps. Return

would not be countenanced. We chose the north
face, finally, feasible. Once high enough,
we made our base camp, followed by Camp One,
Two, Three, and Four, all linked, with traffic back
and forth in ant trails, and at last some sense
of how we might succeed. Yet nothing seemed
assured, where snowscapes stretched, bent, broke, and rose
as alien as the mountains of the moon.

To pitch Camp Five, just two of us went on,
ascending painfully by vertical
attacks with crampons, axes, lines, to reach
long sickle cliffs for the assault. We fixed
our tent that night by pitons. As in dream,
each movement cost tremendously. At dawn,
afraid of frostbite, breathless, with no sleep,
I was an automaton, in a trance.

       ii

We persevered, though; somehow, effort paid
us better while we hoped, and struggled, on.
The final yards lay open, oyster-like.
Strange happiness ran through me—an unknown
possession. But we must not stay, an hour
at most, the weather turning rough, the slope
dissolving, fast. We hastened down, picked up
our gear at Five, then slogged on toward Camp Four,

the only shelter. Half-delirious
by then, I stopped, removed my gloves, and saw
them roll downhill. My partner, crazed with fear,
outpaced me, but got lost and fell—near camp,
by luck; his frantic calls were heard above
the wind. We both had frostbite. Night was worse,
as heavy snow in masses crushed the tents,
and ropes and pitons jerked. That morning fell

instead of rising—terrifying mist
that changed the contours of the scene and closed
perspectives. Staying, though, was folly, since
the premature monsoon was chasing us.
Our small team lost its way across those fields
of snowy nothingness. Towards dark, we plunged,
unseeing, through the surface. In a cave
of ice—miraculous—I found new calm,

convinced it was my grave. An avalanche
awoke us, huddled. Two were snow-blind; boots
could not be seen, nor forced on swollen feet.
The others pulled themselves, by grace, along
the channel we'd come down; I was the last,
the weakest. Why not die, I thought, right there,
surrounded by the finest mountains, skies
(what irony that day) of sapphire blue?

iii

And yet I let myself be coaxed up, pulled
and dragged along. Another avalanche—
a spewing snow volcano—hit us soon
and nearly killed us, wrenching us apart,
suspending me, head down, in a crevasse.
By then my feet were senseless, and my hands
were black, soon bleeding when I had to slide,
by rope, flesh gone, down pitches and couloirs.

The Camp Two doctor took the wounded men
in charge. My greatest dread was of gangrene
and amputation. The retreat meant pain
for all, and surgery for me; despite
his care, successively I lost my toes
and fingers. Too, it was a race against
the water—rivers rising, crossings not
approachable. It took us endless weeks.

Did we torment ourselves for pride? To show
our courage, test our manhood, gain, with height,
the altitude of character? Was it
for France, humiliated, hurt by loss?
At least we did not torture others, just
ourselves as volunteers, unlike the war
and its unearthly wickedness. I think
credentials were at stake, or *mine*. So few

could do it, and no women—although they
possess their own endurance, strength.
The taste of conquest varies, but it's will,
imagination, and desire that drive
us. Then we make, and find, our luck. Thenceforth
I measured man—myself—by what we did
on Annapurna, all of us, and tried
to live as Montaigne counseled: *a propos.*

Charming the Beasts

—2020

The denizens of zoos, here and abroad,
have suffered from withdrawal, in a dearth
of company, all visitors outlawed.
(Like us, they're social creatures, and self-worth

appreciates when mirrored.) Thus, in Cologne,
a pianist, with keyboard, went to call
upon the animals. He played his own
sonata, "by appointment to them all."

Wise elephants, adjusting a great ear,
approached; goats frolicked in delight; giraffes
attended closely; penguins waddled near;
in the aquarium, as if for laughs,

the dolphins leapt and dived. All listened, rapt,
or bounded, climbed, turned circles, swayed—the least,
the great—for happiness; sea lions clapped.
These modern rites and their devoted priest,

an Orpheus, can soothe the savage breast,
the melody, the rhythm like that Lyre
which made the rocks arise, the rivers rest,
waves fall—enduring still, a starry choir.

Thelonius, he's called, a storied name.
His harmonies ring smoothly to our ears
and ripple out, to animals' acclaim.
It's nature, primed, the music of the spheres.

Three Sonnets for Stella

On Restoration of Her Power

Thank God, the power that failed was not your own—
your mind, your sensibility, your art;
mere lighting, cooling, stove, your mobile phone
went out. Not incidental, though—all part

for us of being bodies, flesh and bone,
and needy. On the coastline, where we chart
the hurricanes—fierce winds, great waters blown,
vast floods—how can one moor a feeling heart?

You lived by lanterns, one small fan, and grit,
and ate cold food from cans. Full benefit
is still to come, as poetry lay low,

to keep its counsel. You received, and gave,
good courage, and you learned what signs to save.
The lights are on; the words will overflow.

On Moving for Another

The task is doubled by the circumstance,
and moving's rarely easy. What a year
for you! Two hurricanes; the long mischance
of Covid closing things, dispensing fear;

and then your only brother had a stroke,
across the state. Disabled badly, near
incompetence. The Parcae spun, and spoke,
though; it is done. So now, you'll drive there, clear
his place of furnishings, his books and clothes
(his character), and trap a feral cat
to be expelled from its warm habitat.

(You do not wish the creature dead, God knows.
Enough already.) May we too be moved
by goodness, move for others, and be proved.

In the Great Louisiana Freeze

Your pipes, old wounded soldiers of the frost,
are wrapped; below the house, a lattice gives a bit
of warmth to errant cats. But you have lost
your garden—what was left when one storm hit

after another. Now the power's off—
again!—and inside temperatures fall
by fives and tens in no time! *Philosophe*,
you must be. But you ask, "Lord, is this *all?*"

To be distressed, though, is to be alive.
Before it's dark, get out a match, a candle,
a chafing dish, good china, to contrive

the atmosphere of a delightful meal;
pour wine, of course. There's little you can't handle
with your experience. Serve out your zeal.

Pat Curating His Library

It started with *Tom Sawyer*, from a generous aunt,
of foreign birth but knowing all the better
what the use of books might be for this bright boy,
determined, eager. Decades later, his collection
held a dozen copies, maybe more, comprising
gifts and other favorites, some well-worn:
critical editions, boxed sets with *Huckleberry Finn*
(numerous duplicates of that likewise, in sundry

printings), and translations into German, French,
and other tongues. Plus all the rest of Twain,
Pat's fellow "Show Me" from Missouri, each
a river-man (though Pat, fourteen, was merely
an apprentice deck hand). He bought commentaries
and biographies—enormous tomes—and Twain's own
ramblings, later called "autobiography." All that
made a cluster, never separated in Pat's moves,

up to the move of death and scattering of many books
—ashes of the mind. Other clusters: T. E. Lawrence,
Faulkner, Irving, RLS, Wolfe, Lindbergh, various
odd specimens. Mostly men's authors. But lots
of poetry as well, hard-bound, great names
both British and American, some French, and poets
of our time—Heaney, of course, Sylvia Plath
(hardly in my view, whatever others think, a worthy

name to stand with those of Wordsworth, Byron,
Tennyson, Longfellow, Poe). And history,
explorers! whether on foot, by horse, by sea: the poles,
America, the equatorial latitudes, Near East, the Orient.
Otherwise, Pat's shelves were in no order—never,
perhaps; or such as had obtained once was undone.
He had two books out, always, sometimes
three, in different rooms and chairs. New items,

many, were at hand, but for the older—valued
differently—he often had to search; in doing so,
he rearranged some, made discoveries (!),
found what he had not wanted, necessarily,
but might be just as good, or better. So I see him
standing there, before a bookshelf, reading
sideways down the spines, or taking out
a first book, then a second, checking or comparing,

rectifying misalignment, laying aside a jacket
to be mended or discarded (though he held them
always in a high regard and preserved them carefully
for years—they also should be read, a *paratexte*).
Sometimes I'd ask him for a book, one
we knew he owned—or I would help him look,
turning here, then there. "What's its color?" "Which
edition?"—or he'd find a substitute. I am bereft

of curator, you see, of one who cared tremendously
for books but would have sacrificed
the whole collection for my sake. Now,
I return the favor as I can, bestowing on him
fresh creations—full of his own Irish spirit, often.
I select a gorgeous book of his, leaf through,
and find the makings of new poems and the reason
I should make them, writing, shaping tombs in words.

Blue Carafe

She was a fervent communist, in France,
in '39 and after. Yet she came
from comfort. Guilt? No; happy chance.
It was her daily pleasure to proclaim

allegiance to the Soviet ideal.
A civil servant, with a salary,
her savings, and a pension, she could feel
secure: "Will not the State take care of me?"

It did, and well. She liked rich furnishings,
good clothes, when they were made again, fine wines
(Bordeaux), oak cabinets, old table things
(stiff napkins, china, silver, crystal—signs

of value). She had never married. Half,
at least, of her possessions later crossed
the ocean when she died, the blue carafe
among them—Caribbean blue, embossed

in gold (a floral pattern), narrow neck,
a beveled stopper. Lovely. I like small
remembrances. It reached me through a fleck
of fortune—such events as can befall

the lucky: asked to name from an array—
my friends' inheritance—a favorite piece,
I chose at once. "It's yours." To give away
such honored property is to increase

its worth by friendship, this time twice: for them,
for her. They said she carried everywhere
her party flag, but knew the apothegm
that beauty is as precious as the air.

Two Photographs

Colorado, 1935

A snapshot eighty-six years old, I think,
re-photographed: a couple, almost young,
in summer, with their child. Then, in a blink
of time (it seems), they're merely shades, among

memorabilia. My father wears
a deep-crowned straw; my mother's hair is waved
and short, in thirties style. She's slim. She stares
into the sun; he smiles. My cousin saved

this photo; older, she remembered. Now
it's come to me, who could not understand
the moment. It eludes me still. I bow
to love, to loss, its token in my hand.

California, 1936

Two palm trees, sun, a stylish Chevrolet
with running board, a handsome, well-dressed man
and lovely woman on their wedding day
in Santa Barbara. Their fortunes ran

to happiness, as radiant as here.
She's got dark hair, smart clothes, and Irish wit;
he's clever, with good breeding. Every year
they drove to see the family—a fit

of temperament and blood. Their harmony
endured, until she found him on the floor, a stone.
She grieved. No need for mourning or suttee;
she kept her dresses, and went out alone.

Russian Olive Thicket

—For J. and J.

This is no grove; it's a forest, a *dark wood*, if you wish.
Although the leaves look light—various grays,
pale greens and whites, according to the sun—
they cover limbs and twigs as black as pitch.
As wholes, the trees seem shaped—
domed, rounded globes against the spindly willows

by the river and tall conifers clinging to the mesa.
But behind their leafy screens, they're shadowy naves,
their pillars, vaulting, tracery entangled—
nets and labyrinths, thorny, threatening. Drawn,
we venture in, a sanctum or a dream.
Deeper, darker. No breakthrough to the sky; no end

and no relief. Small clearings let us pause,
three visitors without a guide, pilgrims without progress;
or, perhaps, three spirits. We can barely feel
our feet, gliding, mute. We do not leave
crumbs. Are we shades already, moving
into some mysterious knowledge, moving into ourselves?

Tell the Birds I'm Coming

—For M. and E.

Old friends of mine along Bayou Saint-John
invite me for a visit. Welcome words!
So far, the winter's been quite dismal, wan.
That bayou and its banks are home to birds—

anhingas, pelicans, and cormorants,
blue herons, ducks, all masters at their craft,
their livelihood, their prehistoric dance
of stalking, diving, rising on a draft

of sun-warmed air, or bobbing up, like buoys.
So tell them, please, I'll be there soon, and while
we can, we'll savor the peculiar joys
of birds and friendship, in New Orleans style.

We'll watch them fish, admiring their ease
in swoop and plunge, the iridescent shine
on feathers, watching graceful moves through trees
(live oak and cypress). We'll have coffee, wine,

and lunch on trays in your solarium.
Outside, you'll prune a branch; we'll celebrate
your garden—nature's green curriculum—
and birds, the flying forms of our estate.

Meyer Lemons

Would that my epidermis were so fine!
They're smooth, symmetrical, a lovely shade
of easy yellow with a bit of shine.
It is as though they had been made

for viewing pleasure—ours; they justify
their being by their beauty. Rounder shapes
set off their oval value for the eye—
a simple orange, a plum, or Xeuxis' grapes,

which fooled a bird. The pleasures of their use
await us shortly, since the realm of fruit
is functional (those vitamins! that juice!),
while bearing in itself an absolute.

I'll slice a lemon thin and cut the rind
for zest; we'll keep its image on our mind.

SIX WAR POEMS

Dinant, August 1914

Late June '14: an Austrian archduke died
by an assassin's hand. A pawn, that's all.
The chessboard changed. Alliances and pride
moved pieces toward an end none could forestall.

Mid-August, Feast of the Assumption: war
now two weeks old. In Belgium, on the Meuse,
Dinant had been contested twice before.
This time the Teuton forces would not lose.

French fighters occupied the Citadel,
when Jägers, with machine guns, overcame
them, leaving one-half dead. The stronghold fell
again that very day—a deadly game

foreshadowing the trenches. Germans massed
their troops, secured pontoons. First, raids at night.
The 23rd, they crossed: blast after blast,
grenades and cannon, houses fired, to spite

resistance. In one month, a thousand dead
civilians, pillage, executions, rape,
two libraries in ruins—and ahead
four years of butchery, with no escape.

To what avail were pacts, with Europe, torn,
gouged out, perhaps nine million soldiers killed?
Though time grew late, the peace was never born.
The ancient prophecies are well fulfilled.

At the Keyboard

—In memory of M. B. H.

i

She had resolve, good wrists, long fingers—fine,
light hammers. First, she learned at home, then went
to Montreal for study and did well.
One summer she sailed off to France, to train
at the *Conservatoire américain*
in Fontainebleau. But that was '39. The war
had given a reprieve the year before—
its third—but would not hold its furious dogs

forever. Hitler was not subtle; threats
were constant, rumbling as he played his card,
the Soviet Pact, which sold away the Poles.
Why wait? He staged an incident, and then
attacked. It was September 1st. That meant
the end; she must leave France, if possible.
Abandon masters, models, art! And how,
with trains, ships in disorder, turned aside

or in reserve? By great good chance, and will,
she got a berth aboard the *Île de France*,
the last to leave for North America,
quite overcrowded. Did the music last,
a jewel preserved, like those sewn in the coats
and trousers of the refugees? Did sounds
of panic in the Paris streets persist
among the summer memories, unique?

ii

She did not marry. Having lost to war
a brother, she provided company
to those who'd loved him longest. And she taught
so well, a classroom genie: history,
piano, English, Latin—ligatures
with others, with the true, good, beautiful.
She ironed rough moments, darkness, aging, death,
by habit less than strength of mind. At four

each afternoon, her school tasks put aside
or housework done, she washed her hands, with care
(I see her now), selected scores, and sat
to practice. Beethoven— the "Pathétique,"
the "Tempest," and "The Grand." Or Mozart, Bach,
some Schubert, Schumann, Liszt. For whom? Herself?
Those few around her still, who needed her?
Or shadowy figures listening in the wings,

that jury of the past or the ideal?
In time, nearly alone, she practiced less,
not losing will, but as her knuckles turned
arthritic, knotty; swollen wrists caused pain—
tuberculosis of the bones. Why play?
You cannot raise the sailor from the depths
by song, nor smooth a brow, nor hear again
those chords of happiness before the lamps went out.

Compiègne

—June 2001, June 1940

i

We take the train, a friend and I, northeast
from Paris. Old Compiègne has cobblestones,
fine buildings, souvenirs of war (not least,
an empress's museum), overtones

of failure. First, we visit the château,
have lunch at a café, outdoors, in shade,
then find a taxi driver free to show
us—somber scene—the famous glade.

ii

—It's nineteen-forty, *déjà vu*, the worse
for France: same fight, familiar enemy,
the ritual acts of closure, in reverse;
invasion, refugees, retreat—and obloquy.

The memories hang thick—the armistice
of nineteen-eighteen, with the Kaiser fled,
and Marshal Foch on hand, victorious,
firm, Gallic. This time, Nazi pride, instead.

Surrender must be recognized as shame,
der Führer vowed. He chose the railroad car
where Germany, defeated, signed its name,
the very clearing, to efface the scar

of deep humiliation he had borne.
Defeat ate at his psyche, a disease
that found relief in madness. He had sworn
to humble *Frankreich*, bring her to her knees—

preserving, though, the land of Charlemagne,
of culture, envied long, for his New Order.
He'd go in triumph, gloat, exploit it, drain
its men, seize its resources—no more border—

then reach to England. An Atlantic empire!
—those stubborn Brits, their Churchill and their Channel!
Next, Russia, *Lebensraum*, by reign of fire—
fantastic vision, thousand-year-long annal.

     iii

The Allies' flags displayed, the polished wood
and beautiful design belie the loss
of many millions, fallen for the good
of millions more—a trade with fate, the cross

of all humanity.—Departing, we salute
the suffering, the sacrifice, the gore.
Our guilt is history, the branch, the root.
The tide is washing on a distant shore.

Jean Cassou in Prison

Of mostly Spanish blood, but French, Cassou,
though *homme de lettres*, living, writing well
—translations, essays, novels, poems too—
in '40 started a Resistance cell

his friends and he called "Literary Club."
His means were words—a newssheet, underground.
A state museum served them as a hub.
When the Gestapo threw its seine around

them, he fled south, but later he was caught,
tried, sentenced to a Vichy prison. Might
he have encountered worse? Of course. He thought
of those in Drancy, and the "fog and night"

of camps in Germany, just barely known.
He suffered, though; he could not write—no pen,
no paper, nothing—just cold walls of stone.
Yet language throve somehow—the oxygen

of self. He mined it, underneath his breath—
a first, a second poem, remembering
his father's brilliance and his early death,
old songs his Spanish mother used to sing,

the lines of Valéry, Apollinaire,
and Hugo, protesting—an exercise
at night, in concentration, through despair—
yet charms. The sonnets formed before his eyes

and sounded inwardly; soon others, born
of loneliness, love, loyalty to France,
took shape. He finished thirty-three. To mourn
is pointless now; the poet found his chance

and strung out verses, beads of hope before
the struggle ended—stelae, with the price
of empire paid, like those of the Great War,
enduring evidence of sacrifice.

Normandy, 7 August 1944

They parked their Panzers in a poplar grove,
expecting orders. *Hitlerjungend,* not
supported well, worn down. Montgomery drove
his forces toward them hard, as always. Caught,

then overrun, the SS tried retreat,
but met Canadians, whose countrymen
had perished by a field of summer wheat
as prisoners of Germans at Ardenne.

And each remembered. War is destiny;
to even out the score, the ancient curse—
however crazed and cruel revenge may be—
appears as sacrifice, awaiting worse.

It will not end. The Teutons at La Cambe,
who lie beneath their crosses of basalt,
compose a desperate ideogram,
aligned as for an ultimate assault.

Phoebe, 1944

She looks around, to scan the mountain slope,
the Colorado sky, through stands of spruce
and pine. All's lovely, calm. Brief spasms of hope—
not steady, but the anxious kind, a truce

with fear she barely recognized—assail
her suddenly. Late bits of goldenrod
and scarlet gilia decorate the trail
that rises past the cabin. Blaming God

for dread, for war, is pointless. —Jack's last word
arrived, through San Francisco, weeks ago.
She's looked for letters since. Absurd, absurd!
The fleet's in the Pacific: Borneo,

Malaya, Leyte? Her presentiments
lie low—banked coals; she does not want to think,
but, rather, live somehow in confidence,
a gift to him. Today, her spirits sink,

though. It's ironic: she and Edward crossed
one year to Kobe, toured Japan, made friends,
admired Mount Fuji. All of that is lost,
whatever happens when the horror ends.

She has to stop her trembling, go inside.
It's evening now, and summer's turned to fall.
They'll close the cabin, go to town, and bide
through autumn as they can—and that is all.

—December came, and, finally, the worst
news possible. Jack's ship, attacked, lost power;
afire, flooded, stricken, bulkheads burst,
the engine gone, it sank within the hour.

>

She tried to suffer with him, feel flesh burn,
get lowered, scalded, to the lifeboat, die.
She wept. From such sea there is no return,
What does that burnt oblation signify?

III.

Orchid

—For E. H.

A friend has sent a gorgeous floral gift—
an orchid, of a kind unknown to me.
Of thousands that exist—you get my drift—
how can I guess? I need to know, you see.

For ignorance is contrary to thrift;
it leads to waste, or worse. Economy
in all! Besides, I rarely give short shrift
to curious facts, details, or pleasantry.

The roots aren't set in soil, but funny stuff,
dark green, quite ersatz. Does it live on air?
Or is that compost, nourishing enough

for saprophytic flowers? As it grows,
I'll think "How lovely!"—hoping earth will bear
exotic blooms where I, too, decompose.

Kit Carson in the Navajo Lands

i

Birth: said to be Kentucky. Family: large.
And learning: none at all, if that means books.
The Carsons settled in Missouri near
the Boones, a wilderness. His father died.
Apprenticed to a Franklin saddler, Kit
was bored; he needed something more, which feeds
imagination and resolve. He'd heard the tales
of frontier life, southwestern style, of trade,

exploring, trapping, Indians, Mexicans,
along the trails to Colorado, south
to Taos, Santa Fé, and west. He left
for Independence, aged sixteen, and joined
a wagon train that reached New Mexico,
no longer Spanish, yet an alien land.
The key was work, with skills. He learned to speak
new languages, to cook, to follow tracks.

His changed existence fit him perfectly,
as if some force had bred him for the role.
No giant, though, except in deeds. And those,
year after year, were marvels of good sense,
great fortitude, and luck. Not notches made
for others, since he was not vain; but heart,
endurance, strength. So many treks, with Young,
and Frémont, thrice; so many rendez-vous

with other trappers to sell beaver skins;
so often on the trail to Santa Fé
from Taos or to Bent's Old Fort and back,
the Zuñi lands and west, and Washington.
He was an iron weapon, tool, and shield
for others. He knew Indians, too, the tribes
as far as California, northward—Crows
and Blackfeet, Kiowas, Arapahoes.

     ii

Not all was well—this was a man's life, not
a saint's—nor could it be, in history.
Yet most who curse him now have profited
from such achievements. So he served as guide
for Kearney in the war of '46
against the Mexicans; then, later, he
won honors at Valverde, fighting well
as colonel for the Union forces. Next,

a different struggle, with the Navajos
and the Apaches, able raiders all,
who had resisted efforts to confine
them and would not cease stealing. Carson led
the expedition. Friendly often, kind,
it's said, to women, children, even loved
by Utes, but still he drove the Diné tribe
away, toward east New Mexico, a site

unsuitable for them or anyone.
Just think: their peach trees ruined, felled; sheep seized
(they brought a dollar each) and horses (more);
dead warriors; women fainting on their feet,
and children walking till they died. The boy
Na Nai, born without feet, survived, to be
the leader Nature meant; his mother, gone.
Comanches raided them en route—a curse

beyond endurance. Four years later, those
remaining walked back home to the *Cañón
de Chelly* and land acknowledged theirs. Poor Kit
was ill. Imagine how his dreams whirled round
his head, the cries, the protests, homes destroyed,
and deaths. Perhaps he saw the peach trees still
in bloom, as they had been that awful spring,
their fruit, like lives, mere promise in the mind.

Girls' Weekend

—Late August, 2020

One's Clara; she is sixteen and a half.
Another is her mother, forty-nine.
Then I. The label "girl" will make you laugh.
This poem, and its vision, though, are mine.

(While I like facts, hyperbole has charm;
we use it often—like synecdoche
and oxymoron, surely without harm.)
—The circumstances are bizarre. We three

have met in Nashville, neutral; quarantine
would catch me in New York. At the hotel,
to celebrate, a toast! and *fair* cuisine.
Masks shed, we study menus, order well.

Tomorrow, art—fine Turners from the Tate,
and, at the "Parthenon" (full-sized, a twin
of that in Athens), sixty paintings—great
American examples. Since we're kin,

we can be close, embrace, without a care.
The "boys," at home meanwhile, will entertain
themselves, attend the ailing dog, prepare
their own adventure, manly, when the bane

of this confinement ends. Perhaps they'll hike
the Smokies, snorkel in blue island sea,
take in the Astros, travel west to bike
red desert roads in Utah. We agree:

no hedonism here. Pursuing good,
one learns to be so. Muscles have their place,
like eyes, ears, taste. Well practiced, understood,
in pleasure, as in love and grief, there's grace.

Two Doves

Seated, with an empty coffee cup, I take a glance
outside—the balcony, the early sky. And here two doves
fly in, alighting on the balustrade,
a mated pair (I hope). They pause, turn, look about,
heads a-bob to keep their vision
constant, then investigate what's on a bench

and, fluttering down, peck all around the floor,
a flower pot. Certainly, good omens. It is rare to have
such avian visitors here; my place is very high,
and I put out no food. Still, hope
must spring in columbaceous breasts;
stirring city winds may carry seeds, wild grains,

small berries, insects, even crumbs, dropped
from pizza eaten in the street. The doves have brought
no olive branch—none visible, at least;
there is no flood (right now). But don't we all
need comfort, reassurance, and imagine
messages, beyond these accidents of feathers, flesh?

Chrysanthemums

Gold flowers, says the etymon in Greek.
But many rainbow colors nowadays
evince invention, though the form's antique:
"disk florets," pollened, and the showy "rays."

The plant, perfected long, has been renowned
and loved for three millennia and more,
its fanciers as yet not having found
plump pompons, curling mops to be a bore.

In China, it was first a flowering herb,
developed aptly, trained to play a part
in festivals, symbolic and superb—
one of "Four Gentlemen" in Asian art.

The Japanese, in an encomium
to beauty, borrowed it, put it on their seal,
then named their monarchy "Chrysanthemum,"
a moniker, to me, of rare appeal.

—"All these details! The essence can't be there;
no need to number petals, name each hue,
explain the history, tell how, when, where
chrysanthemums have grown," they say. Quite true.

Perhaps their essence lies in their perfume.
Ah, yes! Described as "herby," of the earth,
unlike sweet floral odors. Or each bloom
may illustrate its soul. Of course!—their worth

is in the eye of the beholder. Or,
in vegetable value: salads, tea.
And in funereal purpose—tributes for
one gone. They flavor wine. A browsing bee

may gain immunity when it enjoys
their presence. Once, they favored love's young flame:
corsages for the girls of yore, and boys
who pinned them on lapels, before the game—

a "festival" (the players were not paid)—
or dinner at the Shamrock or the Rice,
where elegance of dress was interlaid
with intellect. The memory is twice

as precious, now that one of us is dead.
The essence of the flower lies in you,
in us. It will be honored at my head
by friends—its tousled image, its *virtù*.

Remembrance

This is the anniversary of death
for one so close to me that I am still
connected to him, bodily. Each breath
is, as it were, for him, for us. The will

to live, and well, remains, thus; it is part
of his survival. —What a tale! Fate led
the drama, by an arrow through his heart,
allowing us, divided, to re-wed.

Few are so fortunate in bride, in groom,
in error overturned. Though he's called "late,"
the circle was completed; on the loom,
two threads of life are tied. I celebrate.

The Mimosa

What can I say to this girl who hangs
dripping clothes—pennants for a fair
day—on lines strung from my branches,
while her tears fall down in the cracks
of a weathered porch? Is her weeping
some washing of the heart, as regular
as ritual, or the sign of a fresh hurt
that struck a vein? The wind's pulse

is quickening; a tautness attunes us,
as if under way. Well, an old tree
has seen squalls and clearings, ridden
out seasons—mockingbirds tearing twigs,
their fledglings fattened on the flies
in my wake; then, brittle fallen pods,
which scavenger jays break greedily.
Where I was pruned, once, scars still

show; the pollen of a summer dusts
the sea. You might even call me
crippled: three crooked limbs scrape
awkwardly against a railing; yet
I have not retracted a single root,
and my norther-blown pains ease out
when a bird of paradise is reborn
in my blossoms. Will metamorphosis

follow her indignity? See, she bends
to reach her basket, raises her arms
toward the splendid drying sun, and bends
again, to get a nightgown. Later,
when my roots drink of the afternoon
rain, which is readying there, over
the river, will her tears also turn
to sap, somewhere in her soul's garden?

Croquettes

The menu features "Salmon Benedict."
Filet and *oeuf,* no doubt. Still, I inquire.
"Croquettes, and topped with egg." —They won't inflict
on me that foetus! But the words inspire

my appetite; I'll order two, though plain,
and salad, too—a toothsome Caesar, dressed.
"With *béchamel?*" No, thanks. (I shall refrain
from commenting on it.) The final test:

"A single plate, please." Yet here comes a bowl,
wide, deep, in which the salad's nearly lost;
the salmon's on a little dish. The whole
becomes its parts; what's more, the cakes are sauced!

A lesson in mistakes, for what it's worth.
Should we expect perfection on this earth?

At Sea

First, sailing, as a boy—the coast of Maine,
blue waters, lighthouse, currents, rocky bays,
red spruce along the shoreline. To sustain
that life forever—long and happy days,

starred nights—I took up building boats, designed
my own, became a man. Apprenticeship
at sea lasts long, though, if one's lucky: mind
against vast realms of matter. To equip

a vessel, and oneself, means to foresee
distress. —I found it, rode it out, by chance.
My sloop, the *Solo*, met catastrophe—
stove in and sinking—in the vast expanse

of the Atlantic, west of Tenerife,
at night. Debris was not to blame; a whale
perhaps. And dreadful weather. Time was brief
to seize the raft, with bits of gear, a sail,

then launch it, wildly, in a watery hell
of darkness, wind, tremendous waves, a storm
that would not tire—pure wrath. Swell after swell
assaulted me, till I could hardly form

coherent thoughts; sheer desperation led
me somehow to prevail. And thus began
a journey, drifting south and west. Ahead,
eleven weeks of struggling—just a man,

the ocean, nothing else. It's now a blur:
attempting sleep, conserving food, and then
distilling—I, the Ancient Mariner:
saltwater everywhere!. A regimen

for torturers. Try fishing with a spear
too flimsy to endure (it broke off twice);
devouring nasty stuff, which brought me near
to death by vomit. Far from paradise.

—Enough. But I must say how faithfully
birds circled—frigate birds and little terns—
and how dorados, dancing, followed me,
and fed me too. The memory now burns.

You know that I survived. Near Guadeloupe,
three fishermen were out in early light,
with nets and tackle ready, where a group
of my dorados swam. —For me, an awful night,

with little rest. I heard an engine first;
I swivelled on my knees and saw a boat,
three faces, disbelieving. In a burst
of speed, they turned their bow. Thus a remote

encounter came about. Excitedly,
they spoke in Creole; I replied by smiles
and gestures. They were *everything*—the sea,
fraternal after eighteen hundred miles,

and man, its conqueror. *At times.* I knew
my limits. But to live by water, leap
with the dorados!—blue of ocean, blue
of sky! And thoughts, once young, grown older, deep.

Yellow Mustang

Jean's husband liked big toys—some, practical—and he
chose well. An airplane, for a quick hop
over Berthoud Pass down to the Denver airport,
to board a longer flight, or for a weekend
at Lake Powell. Two heavy-duty pick-ups, one
fitted with a snow plow, and a Kenworth 18-wheeler
flatbed, for various male enterprises (hauling,
his balled-root tree activities); a large, luxurious

RV for long road trips or their overflowing guests
(there was a guest house, too); fine wooden boats,
designed, created, kitted out by him for display
and sailing on their pond, or, having traveled
by the Kenworth, on Lake Powell. A houseboat
there, for years—a source of income,
but amusement also. Two more of special note
that paint his character especially. One, a British tank,

tight-turreted, had served in Africa in '42.
He got permission from the county to exhibit it
on Independence Day, driving on U.S. 40—the jewel
of the parade. When, however, the day came, alas,
to sell it (toy-time over), although men
showed interest, how many other wives would let
a husband purchase such a plaything?—The second
was a Chinese junk, berthed in Mexico,

genuine, but not in good condition—a cast-off
from a movie. It was "extra-wide" and "extra-long."
He and a forest ranger friend went to fetch it back.
They chained it to the Kenwood, set out
northeast to Barstow and I-40. Scarcely believing
what they saw, patrolmen of four states put on
their sirens, pulled him over, read his permits,
then, reluctantly, had to let him go. On desert roads,

often reasonably straight, it was easy riding. Imagine,
though, the mountain passes—the approaches, rising
steeply, tighter curves, the hairpin turns!
The junk, however, reached its port and dry dock
for refurbishing. Toys must be treasured
and preserved! Finally, to Lake Powell, via passes,
abrupt descents, twists and bends, and incredulity
once more. All this to say that someone who had borne

four children, kept the house, assisted in the business,
but had no toys, told herself one day
that she deserved one also. A Yellow Mustang
it would be. No air conditioning (not needed much
at their elevations); insurance only for six months a year,
since, unlike the pick-ups, tank, and Kenworth,
it was not well suited to high mountain roads
in snow. So off we went, one summer, she and I, across

the sagebrush slope toward Utah, visiting, then south
to Telluride, on to Durango, on roads notoriously
unfit for junks. But we too got attention—
the car, the "girls," still slim, good hair, in western garb,
plus wit and charm enough for all occasions.
We hummed along, all sunny, sang old songs, laughing.
One day we saw blue herons on the river. *Salut*,
Jean—the toy, the woman, taking joy in life, giving more.

Afghan

I'm rarely keen on handcrafts—appliqué,
for instance, baskets, quilts, embroidery.
Just ask my friends who show off macramé,
knit purses, petit point. No, not for me.

I must of course commend their stuff and act
astonished, first, and then attempt to phrase
my compliments just right, to hide the fact
the work's derivative and just a craze.

It's easy to buy jackets on the rack,
and, in boutiques, distinctive gowns, quite smart.
An open market has good bric-a-brac;
I've seen fine napkins at a discount mart.

"Why go to all that trouble?" is my thought.
It's not about the object, though; the soul
is what's at stake, of course. An item bought
cannot be personal—express one, whole.

My friends must pardon my hypocrisy.
Or, rather, I should change. Their handiwork
is like my poems, right?—a way to *be*,
no odder than my own, a harmless quirk.

ii

This afghan is another thing, a prize.
It was my father's, eighty years ago
or more, made by his mother. In her eyes,
he was unwell, a needy man. To show

both love and art, she exercised such care
that it is beautiful and flawless still.
She used fine yarns, deep dyes, with every square—
four rows of different colors—a quadrille

of contrasts. It was always *there*—design,
Dasein, bright presence, speaking weariness
and comfort both. I cannot now define
my father's daily measure of distress.

We lived one year along the Rio Grande
in far South Texas. Heat and rain and steam
beset us. Was the afghan near at hand,
despite the weather, for a restless dream?

He had it when he learned that Jack was dead,
interred at sea at Leyte Gulf. For each,
I lay it out this morning on my bed.
Are warmth and beauty now beyond their reach?

Great Wind

—Grand Junction, Colorado

This is great country, generally: the Colorado,
the chief river of the west, called the Grand in former days,
joined here by the Gunnison; Grand Mesa
to the east, a mile above the valley floor, wedged
between those two rivers; the "Monument," a ruin
of great age (some 1.7 billion years) looming to the southwest;
the long riffling rows of the Book Cliffs,
ashen, at the southern edge of the Tavaputs Plateau;

and, of course, broad sky, heightened at times
by thunder heads, with an enormous, potent western sun,
sinking about now against a nearly-treeless
landscape. Presently, with dusk, enormous clouds appear,
filling out, looming yonder above the Monument,
where they've been brewing, rising with the yeast of water,
gray, darker gray, then black as lava.
And with them suddenly comes a great wind, swooping

over and around the taluses, heading for the river, charging
the thicket of Russian olive trees, then reaching
the balcony and house, banging shutters, overturning
chairs, carrying off cushions, taking the top
from the hummingbird feeder, slamming doors,
setting a spinner on a whirl. Thunder rumbles, booms
back in a canyon to announce Tonenili,
a benign divinity. No rain falls, however. Such commotion

for so little! Or is it practice, mid-summer exercises
for the monsoon to come? I've seen fierce clouds
of anger on a face; this is, finally, friendlier.
Cool air, an afterthought of bluster, condescends to stay
a while. Doors open up again; but it's too dark
to venture on a cushion-chase. How about a glass
of wine from the vineyards just next door, or higher,
on the mesa, which may catch, after all, the rain, the glorious rain?

Aglaonema

A lovely genus, "Chinese Evergreen."
Mine's of the mottled sort called Silver Bay
—a little present from my friend Christine.
It has, she noted, *feuillage panaché*,

bicolored in this case. Set in a pot
of yellow plastic, which it then outgrew,
transplanted neatly now, it takes its lot
as happy, flourishing as if it knew

it was admired. Don't mock me out of hand:
if plants emit an ultrasonic scream
when injured; if a heavy-metal band
makes rubber trees recoil, then it would seem

they might appreciate affection, care,
responding to a touch. Mimosas live
quite differently from us, but on the air
and light, and sentient, as they take and give.

Cells seen by an electron microscope,
men on the moon, and soon perhaps on Mars:
nothing's so strange that we cannot have hope.
We'll harness messages among the stars,

collect them, analyze and read their codes,
send back replies in ours; we'll find the sense
in subtle signals proffered by green modes—
great mysteries and small, in confluence.

A Call from Porlock

Oh, no, I haven't taken opium,
nor hashish. And not even alcohol,
so early. But the man from Porlock's come
(or woman, this time) anyway—a call

by telephone, a modern mode. "Hello,
hello! I tried to get you Saturday."
(I did not answer then.) A vapid flow
of endless talk ensues. (Please, go away!

A poem's on my mind, words half in place.)
What can I say? It's better to talk now
and get it over, I suppose. I brace
myself, take off my glasses; yet, somehow,

the mood's not right. She loves the theater,
its ambiance. What shows she will attend,
or did, the travel, dates—all such recur;
directors, costumes, casting; with which friend;

and where they'll rendez-vous each night and dine;
her memories of last year, when she met
a famous actor. —I reply, "I'm fine,"
when she inquires, finally. Why fret?

Just tune her out, or, rarely, say "Yes, yes."
Some forty minutes pass, with more details
on plans and past performances. I guess
I should not let myself go off the rails.

To nudge her toward a closure, I remind
her, gently, of the time. "The hours do seem
to fly, don't you agree?" Not too unkind.
At last, we say goodbye. Back to the dream

that was the poem? But the dream may change.
Attentive to our lapses, time will slip
into disguise, leave changelings, rearrange
an image, play with an emotion, clip

the wings of thought. Poor Coleridge never found
again the interrupted pleasure scene,
the dome, the span of Kubla's fertile ground.
Yet certainly his inner eye had been

affected. Did the damsel still not sing?
More beautifully perhaps than if he'd heard
without an interval. A pause may bring
new music, or the necessary word.

Hatch Chiles

No clouds; it's near 100 Fahrenheit, as we've driven
through this September day along I-25, south from Colorado,
down toward Texas. At a picnic place not far
from Raton Pass, we had an early lunch, admiring,
eastward, cones of old volcanoes, green against blue haze.
On the road again, we turned off soon, near Watrous,
crossed the Mora River (lofty cottonwoods),
wandered around to look for traces (few, in fact) of a poet

born there. (Fewer still of those.) The other traffic moved
at 70 or 80, in a dense armada, as the road
neared Santa Fe, where it joined the great rift valley
of the Rio Grande. On through Albuquerque to Socorro,
its unearthly minerals visible. A well-known
speed trap, too. En route, a second rest-and-picnic stop.
(We needed succor.) "Walking Sands," it's called
—walking with the wind. A curious structure, all dark wood,

prison-like. Two warnings set the tone. One, in the "facilities,"
said tuberculosis was a present, growing danger
in New Mexico. Once, the place was known by sufferers
and doctors from the north for "Cure with culture."
The second notice, by the walkways,
warned us to beware of rattlesnakes. Not very friendly, eh?
On such territory, I wear ankle boots; but one cannot
stop breathing. Still sound, we hope, we leave on what will be

a last, long lap. *Very* long. The heat's increased, of course,
with afternoon full on us. I've been at the wheel
this long while, facing white light: Pat, older than I
and often ill, tires easily. But I'm the one who's weary now.
We find an exit ramp, near Hatch, the chile capital
of New Mexico, perhaps the world. No town, though, here,
and no good place to stop, really—
just a local road among fields. We pull off, get out,

stretch, and walk a bit. The scene is chiles, chiles everywhere,
all soaking up the sun. Throughout the valley,
we have spied, behind coyote fences of *latillas*,
hanging clusters of red peppers—*ristras*—functional
and beautiful, along the porches of adobe houses,
bright against the brown. In the field, the ripening chiles,
half-concealed, are dark green, to be picked
at once, or left to turn blood-red. Pat says he's ready

to drive on, not fearing glare, the traffic in Las Cruces,
even the downtown streets of Old El Paso.
In my mind I will see *ristras* reddening a doorway
leading into shadow, or, banner-like, displayed in welcome
close to sandstone steps, a path, and heart-shaped leaves
and yellow blossoms of hibiscus. I already taste the pungency,
the sharp and penetrating flavor of the peppers,
holding for years the heat of soil and sky—life in burning joy.

A Note to One Deceased

You know I've sold my little summer place
in Colorado, purchased as a get-
away from heat and hurricanes, a grace.
(The dreadful winds and flooding that beset

New Orleans cannot reach so far.) And when
we married, it was *ours*—our balcony
and tree, our view on life, a regimen
of love, delight. But you've been gone, now, three

full years, and reasonable modes must rule.
My father's fine idealism lives in me,
as firm as his was; but he was no fool,
nor I. I vote for practicality,

and recognize, inevitably, change
in everything. *Fini, les longs voyages*
toward shimmering rainbow mesas and the range
of picket mountains. They were not mirage;

we prospered on the *mouelle sustantifique*—
—the marrow of that journey—for our eyes,
continuing all summer by Pike's Peak,
a studied show, yet always a surprise.

You took your genius with you there; it stays,
perhaps, to follow morning shadows, feel
a storm inhabit you, see sunset blaze.
You also were consumed by the ideal.

From *The Hours of Catherine of Cleves*

1. *Saint John the Baptist*

This is the wilderness of fasting, prayer—
a rugged landscape, marked by rocks and caves—
and of the crying voice which will declare
the coming of One mightier, who saves.

Emaciated, clad in cloak and hide
(the beast's head visible), pale face, raw hand,
the prophet waits at sunset, to abide
until the time is full across the land.

He holds a bannered staff to represent
the Resurrection; in his arms, the Lamb
of God is cradled, shoulder bleeding, spent—
the Son begotten of the great I AM.

2. *Saint Peter Bestowing the Holy Ghost*

An open *tempietto* holds the scene:
rib-vaulted ceiling, columns, land
and forking road beyond, then sky, marine,
a ship at anchor. On Saint Peter's hand

a dove is posed. He reaches to bestow
the Spirit on one kneeling man, while three
await the holy gift. Their faces show,
with patient attitude, deep faith and piety.

Two graybeards at the left look on; a third,
less gnarled, may be a skeptic. Past the frame,
strange, fleshy plants, like squid, are linked. The bird
of Heaven can hallow all, a living flame.

3. Saint Anthony the Great

The bearded saint, in hooded cape and pale
dalmatic, holds a sturdy cane, a bell
in hand. He does not lean, but may be frail.
He knew temptation and the pains of hell.

But these are not the wilds; he stands before
a verdant landscape, pleasant hills, and towers.
At left, an edifice with open door,
a belfry, orange, and bell, which rings the hours

for Catherine. Beyond a yellow gate
and archway, formed of trees, their branches curled,
a garden calls; she would not hesitate
to see there the salvation of the world.

4. Saint Gertrude

The patroness of those beset by mice
and rats, she stands before red tapestry.
Blue floor tiles feature her preferred device:
crude mousetraps, set to spring. Her sanctity

is symbolized in halo, shepherd's crook,
the habit of an Augustinian nun,
and downcast eyes, to read her open book.
Still, mice *will* play. Her work is never done:

to challenge pestilence and sin, and pray,
as others feed the oxen, gather sheaves.
—A demon thief, below, has seized the day,
among motifs of arbuscules and leaves.

5. *Saint Vincent of Saragossa*

His attributes are few—a book, a rod
with three large hooks. But it cannot convey
the tortures, multiple, endured for God—
the rack, a gridiron, burnt flesh wrenched away.

Portrayed in deacon's vestments, Vincent shows
no fear. He does not see the butterflies
that form the border. Why the artist chose
them is not clear; they do not symbolize

his work. Arranged along a looping vine
with berries, leaves, and scrolls, they make a wreath.
Red admirals and cabbage moths entwine—
one marked, though, by a death's head underneath.

6. *Saint Dorothy*

With flowers in her hair and holding fruit,
the virgin saint of Caesarea lifts
some unknown tool of torture. Her repute
is based on these, her martyrdom, her gifts.

The central plane, ornate, is flat; but bold
perspective, nascent, with its angled lines,
creates a deepened border—leaves of gold
and spiraled latticework with climbing vines.

Below, a scene from Paradise: low wall,
two music-making angels, and a well
whence flow two rivers. Peaceful. But the Fall
awaits mankind: temptation, exile, hell.

7. Saint Nicholas

No banderole along the edge, no chain;
instead, a deckled ivory velum, curled,
resembling clouds. The corners are profane:
in each, three monstrous moons, a lunar world

of greedy faces. On a starry ground,
dark blue, the saint is framed in bishop's dress,
with miter, crozier, chasuble; around
his head, a light. He lifts his hand to bless

imperiled seamen, as he gave, in gold,
his charity to women, to endow
them, saving them thereby from being sold
as prostitutes. What anguish for him now.

8. Saints Cornelius and Cyprian

These clerics, although both of great repute,
and friends, could not be always in accord.
They stand together, each with attribute
(tiara, papal cross-staff; mitre, sword),

one garbed in green, one blue. They occupy
the central panel; but the sides upstage
them, representing to the favored eye
one bird perch, birds, and seven styles of cage.

What workmanship, what ingenuity!
—fine artistry, fine functional design.
Are they for pleasure—Catherine's decree?
Are they for wounded creatures, mercy's shrine?

9. Saint Lucy

She is already what she will become.
In crimson cape, her neck pierced by a sword,
she holds the palm of peace and martyrdom—
both suffering and glory, her reward.

The striking textile pattern, a rosette,
recurs in hues of amethyst and jade,
suggesting jewels, perhaps an amulet
for Christians. At the edge, it is replayed

in *ombré* tones of dark and lighter gray—
a girdle or a necklace, linked in gold,
with tags marked *Luciae Virginis*. Pray.
The artisan creator says "Behold."

10. Saint Alexis

A wooden ladder is his only his sign.
He wears a *houppelande* of lavender,
rose cape. A colored background (the design
in white) completes the scene. These themes recur.

In youth, he gave away his wealth, left Rome,
a beggar pilgrim—no one, with no name,
save faith. Long after, on returning home,
he was not recognized. —Below the frame,

a ladder, alcove, bed. He would remain
there nearly twenty years, a saintly space
for no one. But beneath the counterpane
of scarlet beat humility and grace.

11. *Saint James Major*

His journey is a Christian's paradigm.
With staff, pouch, cockle shell, the fisherman
is on the road to Spain, in sacred time,
a pilgrimage that never will be done,

until the end. There's pleasing symmetry,
God's ideal landscape being without flaw:
two winding roads, hills, castles, greenery—
both garden and the city John foresaw.

They are to come. But meanwhile, the divine
appears among us, pilgrims of belief,
recurring in the bas-de-page design
of priest and widow, consolation, grief.

12. *Saint Cecilia*

She's aureoled, attired in green and red.
Eschewing her most famous quality—
her clavichord, the hope of song—instead,
she has adopted holy falconry.

Her left hand, gloved, supports the hawk; she feeds
it daintily. Greek keys adorn the tile;
the crimson background hanging bleeds,
where hawk and boy disport in avian style.

The feathers in the border do all birds
much honor. Dark gold letters in relief
along the shaft may serve for latent words;
three dove-winged lures suggest a love motif.

13. Saint George Killing the Dragon

The horse and rider dominate the field,
dark green. The dragon, lizard-like, impaled,
lies supine; George's banner, cross, and shield,
his lance, the horse's prancing, have prevailed.

Their witness is a princess, kneeling, crowned,
at left. Hands clasped in prayer, she holds a small
white lamb. A city occupies the ground
beyond, at right, with towers, Norman wall.

The triumph rids the land of something base.
The curlicues and flowers that adorn
the border illustrate its native grace.
They frame a virgin and a unicorn.

14. Christ at Emmaus

The room is set apart, with only three
at table: Luke; the Stranger; Cleopas.
They have been served, but pause; for, suddenly,
while one takes meat, and one lifts up his glass,

they recognize the third, the holy bread
that He is breaking for them, as, just days
before, He broke his body. He was dead,
but sups with them tonight. A farewell phrase

from Matthew, *nunc et semper*, runs below;
Luke's words, above, recount the scene for us.
His halo shines, conflating the tableau
of human time with God's own, glorious.

Endnotes

"Mackenzie in the Western Range." Details on Sir Alexander Mackenzie's journey (1793) and the territory come from Vilhjalmur Stefansson, ed., *Great Adventures and Explorations*, new revised edition (New York: Dial Press, 1947, 1952) and *Webster's New Geographical Dictionary* (1972).

"Grace King on the Bayous." In Louisiana, General Benjamin Butler was given the nicknames "Beast Butler" and "Spoons Butler" (an allusion to his liking for silverware). The phrase in stanza 2 "now / of high estate" recalls the improved fortunes of many women (collaborators) in France during the Nazi occupation.

"Logan, As We Said…" The use of echoes may remind readers of Christopher Smart's poem on his cat Jeoffry, although the form of the poem and pattern of repetition are entirely different.

"Fourteen Modern Poems in the Chinese Mode." Whereas classical Chinese poetry is generally organized in rhymed couplets, rhyming on the even-numbered lines, the standard English translations, by Arthur Waley and others, do not use rhyme. An exception to this norm is found in those by Jonathan Chaves, *Cloud Gate Song: The Verse of Tang Poet Zhang Ji* (Warren, CT: Floating World Editions, 2006). See his prologue on the subject of Chinese prosody and his use of rhyme. The present poems, done in the Chinese manner but original, echo Waley's example in being unrhymed. The frequent use of enjambment here contrasts with the end-stop lines characteristic, with some exceptions, of classical Chinese poetry.

"Grace King Abroad." Sources of information include my *Louisiana Creole Literature: A Historical Study* (2013) and Miki Pfeffer, ed., *A New Orleans Author in Mark Twain's Court: Letters from Grace King's New England Sojourns* (2019). Of Florence, Mark Twain said that Dante, forced into exile, should have been pleased to leave it. Clara (1874-1962), one of the three Clemens daughters, was an accomplished pianist. The two other daughters, Suzy and Jean, died in their twenties. Olivia likewise predeceased her husband.

"For a Champion." Along with a particular poem of mine and my general positions, the offending critic attacked nature poetry.

"Tate Britain." Two outstanding Palladian churches in Venice are San Giorgio Maggiore (nave) and Il Redentore.

"Bloody Marys." [*Sic*], which underlines the *franglais*, is part of the line—that is, the syllable count—and must be placed as it is to preserve the iambic meter.

"Annapurna." This poem is based on the best-selling account *Annapurna: Conquest of the First 8000-Metre Peak*, trans. Nea Morin and Janet Adam Smith (London: Reprint Society, 1952), by Maurice Herzog, leader of the expedition. In 1950, for the first time, the Nepalese government gave permission to a team to climb either Annapurna and Dhaulagiri, slightly higher. A restrictive condition was that the team be entirely French. After arrival, weeks were lost as the men tried in vain to locate approaches to the latter peak, whence the delayed choice of Annapurna. All the camps below Five were manned until the post-conquest retreat. That lengthy ordeal, on foot or, for the two wounded men, carried first by other climbers, then by porters, is covered only briefly here. It lasted from 3 June until 6 July, when they finally reached a train line. Using, doubtless, diaries and perhaps additional records, Herzog dictated the account from his bed in the American Hospital in Paris. After his narrative appeared, controversy arose concerning his veracity. (By prior agreement, his fellow climbers were not allowed to publish their own stories until five years had passed.) Critics found his version self-serving and accused him of being unfair to his companions, one in particular. Accusations of such purported bias may, of course, themselves be skewed and prejudicial. A political motive may have inspired some criticism; Herzog was a Gaullist politician.

"Charming the Beasts." The pianist is Thelonius Herrmann.

"Three Sonnets for Stella." Electricity was restored to Stella Nesanovich's house in Lake Charles three weeks after Hurricane Laura hit (2020). The second hurricane was Delta, which took off again a portion of rooftop repaired after Laura. The third sonnet alludes to the two storms. During the great freeze (2021), temperatures in her house, drafty, like many old Louisiana dwellings, plunged to freezing.

"Pat Curating His Library." After my husband's death, I sold, as he had asked me to do, the condo where we lived—too large for me, as he knew—and most of its contents, and returned to a smaller one we owned. Hence the necessary dispersal of thousands of his books.

"Dinant, August 1914." Declarations of war date from the 1ˢᵗ of August. Germany invaded Belgium on the 4ᵗʰ. The first two German attacks on Dinant were by small units, with few casualties. In the coup de main, 21-23 August, nearly seven hundred civilians, including women and children, were killed, many deliberately. The libraries destroyed are those of Dinant and Louvain. See my poem "Burning in Louvain," in *Breakwater*.

"At the Keyboard." In 1914, Sir Edward Grey said, "The lamps are going out all over Europe." The phrase applies equally well to events preceding immediately the conflict of 1939. The phrase thus links the two wars here, obliquely, as they are in the following poem and historically. See the next note and also that for "Phoebe."

"Compiègne." The glade or clearing (*clairière*) is located in the forest outside of Compiègne, near the village of Réthondes. The empress mentioned is Eugénie de Montijo, the wife of Louis-Napoleon (Napoleon III); the "failure" is the French defeat at Sedan in 1870 in the Franco-Prussian War. The Second World War is judged generally by historians as a prolongation of the earlier; indeed, at the time (1919) many observers predicted it. The carriage is a copy. The original, built by the Compagnie des Wagons-Lits and used by Marshal Foch in the Great War, was seized by the Germans and taken to Berlin, where it was displayed in a museum. It is no longer in existence. It may have been destroyed during the bombing of Berlin, or perhaps deliberately destroyed by the SS.

"Jean Cassou in Prison." The cell, an early one, was officially the "Alain-Fournier" society, after the novelist who died in battle in 1914. Cassou and his friends later joined the important Resistance group based at Le Musée de l'Homme. Arrested in December 1941 for Resistance activity in Toulouse, where he had gone upon fleeing Paris, too dangerous, Cassou was put into solitary confinement. Only near the end of his prison time was he allowed writing materials, with which he recorded the poems. He was released but then interned for some time in a camp run by the Surveillance du Territoire, an espionage service. In August 1944, at the time of the liberation of Toulouse, his car ran into a German column; two of his companions were killed and, in a coma, he was left for dead, but then rescued and hospitalized. That month, before the Liberation of Paris, his *Trente-trois sonnets composés au secret* were published, under the pseudonym Jean Noir, by a clandestine press. The phrase "fog and night" is a variant of the French "Nuit et brouillard," or, in German, "Nacht und Nebel." The reference is to a decree promulgated by Heinrich Himmler in 1941, alluding to handling of subversives arrested in their home countries, who were to be deported and then simply vanish. The novelist Jean Cayrol, who barely survived imprisonment (for Resistance activity) at the Mauthausen camp, near Linz, used the expression in his script for a film of the same name by Alain Renais (1956). Paul Valéry's principal collection of poems is titled *Charmes*.

"Normandy, 7 August 1944." The German unit was 12th SS Panzer Division, Waffen SS, composed largely of *Hitlerjungend* and officers gathered from remnants of other units. Although young, or perhaps because of it, they were, apparently, fanatics. The encounter sketched in stanza 1 was part of the Falaise battle. The unit had seen action on 7-8 June at the Abbaye d'Ardenne, near Caen, where twenty or so Canadians held as prisoners of war were shot in the head; some were killed in the abbey garden, others right outside. They were among a total of some 156 Canadian POWs believed to have been executed by that unit. After the war, the commander, Kurt Meyer, taken prisoner, was found guilty by a Canadian court of war crimes; his death sentence was later commuted. The abbey is set among wheat fields. The garden contains a modest memorial to the victims. See my poem "In the Abbey d'Ardenne," in *Places in Mind*. The location is not to be confused with the Ardennes. Of the several German cemeteries for war dead, La Cambe is the largest.

"Phoebe, 1944." The ship is the USS *Johnston*, a destroyer, which fought heroically and achieved a great deal before sinking in the Battle of Leyte Gulf, 23 October. The central figure here is the author's grandmother, Phoebe Elliott Hill. The lost sailor is her son John Elliott Hill, a lawyer who had been successful enough to argue a case before the Colorado Supreme Court but, in the circumstances of the Depression, found attorney's work unpleasant and joined the Navy after declaration of war.

"Kit Carson in the Navajo Lands." The name *Chelly* is pronounced, approximately, *Shay*. *Cañón* takes the Spanish pronunciation here, of course. Carson went on his first real trapping expedition with Ewing Young (1794-1841). The Long Walk of the Navajos took place in 1864, beginning, according to some authorities, in April. Sources of information used for this poem include Laura Adams Armer, *Dark Circle of Branches* (New York: Longmans, Green, 1933); Ferol Egan, *Frémont: Explorer for a Restless Nation* (New York: Doubleday, 1977); LeRoy R. Hafen, ed., *Fur Trappers and Traders of the Far Southwest* (Glendale, CA: Arthur H. Clark, 1968); LeRoy R. Hafen and Ann W. Hafen, *Old Spanish Trail* (Glendale, CA: Arthur H. Clark, 1954).

"Chrysanthemums." The "Four Gentlemen," in order of the seasons they represent (first in Chinese, subsequently in other East-Asian art), are the plum blossom, orchid, bamboo, and chrysanthemum. (This seasonal order, beginning, unusually, with winter, is dictated by the euphony of the Chinese words.) The phrase "number petals" is an allusion to Dr. Johnson's admonition (in *Rasselas*) not to number the streaks of the tulip. In France, Belgium, and certain other European countries, chrysanthemums are uniquely for funereal purposes. In New Orleans they are used widely thus, especially on All Saints' Day. In connection with bees, it should be observed that they may frequent chrysanthemums and take the nectar, and it is believed that their immunity to mites, an enemy, is enhanced through contact with the natural insecticide in the blossoms. But spiders, a second natural enemy, lurking deep, pose a risk. The Shamrock and Rice, Houston hotels at mid-century, were the settings for many college dinners and dances, as late as the 1960s.

"Croquettes." See my poem "Eggs," in *On the North Slope*.

"At Sea." This poem is based on Steven Callahan's *Adrift: Seventy-six Days Lost at Sea* (Boston: Houghton Mifflin, 1986).

"Yellow Mustang." The junk was part of a fleet of boats used for the movie *Lady Luck* (1975).

"Afghan." See "At the Keyboard" and "Phoebe, 1944" in this collection.

"Hatch Chiles." The poet is Peggy Pond Church, whose father, Ashley Pond, moved to New Mexico from the east as a young man and took up ranching. See my study *Southwestern Women Writers and the Vision of Goodness* (Jefferson, NC: McFarland, 2016).

"A Note to One Deceased." This poem was composed in summer 2020. The phrase "Fini, les longs voyages" is quoted from my poem "Stockholm, June 2000," from *On the North Slope*. (Those who know French will recognize that the adjectival participle *fini* is, like others, invariable when it precedes the noun.) The quotation pertains to the aviator-writer Jules Roy. It goes farther back, however, to Alain-Fournier's novel *Le Grand Meaulnes* (1913), where it refers wistfully to Meaulnes's wanderings. The expression *mouelle sustantifique*, or substantial marrow, comes from Rabelais, "Prologue to the First Book."

"From *The Hours of Catherine of Cleves*." This group of fourteen poems continues, as it were, a group of eight I drew from the same medieval source. Originally published in *Modern Age*, they were collected in *A Memory of Manaus*. Those in the first set are subtitled "Suffrages"—scenes of saints' lives. This set includes a tableau to which the term would not apply, since, although Saint Luke is a participant, Christ himself is depicted; it is "Supper at Emmaus" (here retitled "Christ at Emmaus"), from Thursday Hours of the Sacrament—Vespers. See *The Hours of Catherine de Cleves*, with introduction and commentaries by John Plummer (New York: George Braziller [1964]).

About the Author

Catharine Savage Brosman is Professor Emerita of French at Tulane University and Honorary Research Professor at the University of Sheffield. She is the author of more than a dozen collections of poems and several chapbooks, published by the University of Georgia Press, Louisiana State University Press, Mercer University Press, Shotwell Publishing, and other presses. For more than five decades her verse has appeared frequently all over America, especially in the *Sewanee Review*, the *Southern Review*, and *Modern Age*. Poems of hers have been anthologized and featured on the radio and sites such as Poetry Daily and American Life in Poetry. Translations of her poems have come out in the Paris monthlies *La Nouvelle Revue Française* and *Europe*. In addition, she has published short fiction (*An Aesthetic Education and Other Stories*, 2019), and three collections of personal and cultural essays. Her scholarly studies include eighteen volumes on French authors and four in the field of American regional literature. Since 2007 she has been poetry editor of *Chronicles: A Magazine of American Culture*.